NORMAL GETS YOU NOWHERE

NORMAL GETS YOU NOWHERE

KELLY CUTRONE

with MEREDITH BRYAN

HarperOne
An Imprint of HarperCollins*Publishers*

HarperOne

FIRST EDITION
Interior design by Laura Lind Design

Library of Congress Cataloging-in-Publication Data is available.

ISBN 978–0–06–205979–6

11 12 13 14 15   RRD(H)   10 9 8 7 6 5 4 3 2 1

For Ava,
my mother,
and the Universal Mother

Do not simply believe what you hear just because you have heard it for a long time.

Do not follow tradition blindly merely because it has been practiced in that way for many generations.

Do not be quick to listen to rumors.

Do not confirm anything just because it agrees with your scriptures.

Do not foolishly make assumptions.

Do not abruptly draw conclusions by what you see and hear.

Do not be fooled by outward appearances.

Do not hold on tightly to any view or idea just because you are comfortable with it.

Do not accept as fact anything that you yourself find to be logical.

Do not be convinced of anything out of respect or deference to your spiritual teachers.

You should go beyond opinion and belief. You can rightly reject anything which when accepted, practiced, and perfected leads to more aversion, more craving and more delusion. They are not beneficial and to be avoided.

Conversely, you can rightly accept anything which when accepted and practiced leads to unconditional love, contentment and wisdom. These things allow you time and space to develop a happy and peaceful mind.

This should be your criteria on what is and what is not the truth; on what should be and what should not be the spiritual practice.

—From the *Kalama Sutta*, The Buddha

CONTENTS

INTRODUCTION

I'm not going to change the way I look or the way I feel
to conform to anything. I've always been a freak. So I've
been a freak all my life and I have to live with that, you
know. I'm one of those people.

—John Lennon

I was always fascinated by people who are considered
completely normal, because I find them the weirdest of all.

—Johnny Depp

One day last spring, I got a call from my publishing company. They were ready to talk book number two. *What?* I thought. *Book number one just came out three months ago! Are these people on crack?* It turns out my editor didn't just want any second book—she wanted me to rewrite the Ten Commandments! By now I was *sure* she hated me. She was probably envisioning me writing things like, "Thou shalt have sex with whomever you want, whenever you want, wherever you want." (And actually, that is a commandment I'd write.) Even though every fiber in my being—as well as my years of professional experience—screamed, "NO!" I decided to give the Commandments a once-over, just to make sure I wasn't missing anything.

I mean, have you read them lately? I pulled them up online, and I have to say number nine really got me going:

> You shall not covet your neighbor's house; you shall
> not covet your neighbor's wife, or his manservant, or

3

his maidservant, or his ox, or his ass, or anything that is your neighbor's.

Oh, you know, *anything that is your neighbor's*—his ox, his ass, *or his wife!* As I suspected, I was not down with this. I told my editor I would respectfully pass on rewriting the Ten Commandments, but that I'd love to write a second book, thank you very much.

And this time I started with the assumption that you already know that 90 percent of what we're seeing around us and being asked to do and agree with is complete and utter bullshit, whether it's called "commandments" or the Law. I'm writing for all of you who have ever stood up against the falsity that's been labeled truth and shoved down our throats as well as anyone who still aspires to. But most of all, this book is for people who want to find personal fulfillment and success in their career, but *also* live in a world full of unique, creative, expressive individuals who march to the beat of the Divine's drummer, agreeing on things like basic human rights and the need to end suffering.

Basically, this book is for freaks. In my opinion, we need to raise an army of supertalented uberfreaks if we're ever going to really change the world—since it's only freaks who ever have. Look at Steve Jobs, Helen Keller, Rosa Parks, Vivienne Westwood, The Mother, Nelson Mandela, Indira Gandhi, Benjamin Franklin, Bono, Vincent Van Gogh, Paco Rabanne, Che Guevara, Amelia Earhart, Leonardo Da Vinci, Pope Joan, Leonard Cohen, Beethoven, Albert Einstein, Joan of Arc . . . well, you get the picture. How many of these people followed anyone else's rules? Could any of them possibly be considered anything *close* to normal?

Let's pause for a moment to see what Merriam-Webster has to say about "normal":

nor-mal: **2 a:** according with, constituting, or not deviating from a norm, rule, or principle; **b:** conforming to a type, standard, or regular pattern; **4 a:** of, relating to, or characterized by average intelligence or development.

Duh. I rest my case. Who wants to be that?

By now you probably know that I have little patience for the teachers, parents, bosses, and even friends who tell everyone they need to sit quietly and fit in. History is full of successful, world-changing people who did *not* fit in and were definitely *not* normal. Instead of changing themselves to accommodate the status quo or what others thought they should be, these people put a spotlight on their differences—and changed humanity in the process. Is it possible that the so-called normal people, the ones doing things the way the majority of people are doing them, are the crazy ones? I mean, have you ever visited Wal-Mart at around eleven on a Friday night? It is one of the scariest biospheres of zombie "Thriller" normalcy I've ever seen!

I've now been working for over twenty-five years—longer, if you count the snow-shoveling business I started at the age of ten up in Syracuse, which employed four other kids (okay, two were my brother and sister)—and I've interviewed thousands of people for an array of positions. To be honest, I dread every so-called normal person who walks through the door. The mantra that always plays in my head is, *Same ole, same ole.* It's time we started seeing words like "kooky," "abnormal," "crazy," "eccentric," and "freak" as what they are: *character differentiation*. I know you don't feel normal, so why are you trying to act it and prove to everyone you are?

And once you agree you're actually as distinctive and individual as your thumbprint— even if you've been programmed to behave in "normal" ways—*then* what? How do we use our specific eccentricities to make a difference in ourselves, our immediate community, our chosen field of employment, and ultimately the world? I happen to believe that the days of going to work all day, making a shitpot of money, and blowing it all on sex, drugs, and rock 'n' roll—or any of the other things on this planet that exist to make us feel full and complete—are over.

Please don't misconstrue this. I want you to have a fucking great time. But I think it's absolutely essential for you to know you are sacred, magical, and special, to nurture that truth *and unleash it into the world*. That's right. I want you to fuck this earth with your energy. It's about time we stood for something real. I'm suggesting that what is real is *you*. That means your message and purpose in this world will be different than mine, and that the more you really start to know yourself and gain life experience—when you really start to crack yourself open—you'll naturally find it.

What do you have to say? What in this world are you called to fight for?

Is it human rights, peace, or polar bears and nature? Is it, as it is for me, young women and gay men? If you aspire to be yourself, and I hope you do, things like education, self-confidence, and learning to communicate and defend yourself are superimportant tools. The truth of the matter is, if you want to find success outside the norm, you really have to fine-tune your skills and become incredibly good at what you do.

If you're going to get in the ring, babe, you better know how to box.

Take me, for example. I'm really glad I'm allowed to wear all black and no makeup while working in the fashion industry, but I think the only reason I'm allowed to do that is because I tend to get the job done.

And remember, the people who are most cherished and revered on this earth are sometimes the same people who are most ostracized, misunderstood, and hated. From Jesus to Abraham Lincoln to Vincent Van Gogh to Jane Fonda, it's obvious that people don't like people who rock the boat or even *row* the boat, let alone park it in their driveway or on the lawn. They like people who sit quietly in the boat—who have paid in advance for their ticket and don't say fuck. I believe that when we see people acting "bizarrely" in this world, conjuring "odd" ideas, and talking "crazy," we should stop for a second before being so quick to judge; perhaps we should even move toward them.

And when we have these ideas ourselves, maybe we should examine or draw them out like a beautiful piece of ribbon candy, instead of stifling them because we think others won't get it. After all, so much of what we say or don't say, and what we do or don't do, is dictated by what others have told us or what people may think of us. This is not how we should be living—measuring ourselves against the mundane. As you have your own Divine revelations and nurture your own intuition,

I want you to share them with the world. And don't retreat or feel bad if no one gets it at first. Because, let's face it, you can only *hope* they don't get it. This will give you an edge, otherwise known as a patent or a trademark opportunity. In commerce, in literature, and in life,

Normal gets you nowhere.

ONE

COMFORTABLY NUMB

The media's the most powerful entity on earth.
They have the power to make the innocent guilty and
to make the guilty innocent, and that's power. Because
they control the minds of the masses.
—Malcolm X

All of us who professionally use the mass media are the
shapers of society. We can vulgarize that society, we can
brutalize it. Or we can help lift it to a higher level.
—Bill Bernbach

These days, American life is pretty much set up to allow us to feel as little as possible. We've been desensitized by the thousands of choices capitalism presents us on a daily basis: five hundred TV channels, seventy brands of cereal in the grocery store, sixteen different vitamin drinks, forty-seven brands of jeans. In the words of Pink Floyd, we've become "comfortably numb." While horrible things happen all over the world, we spend a lot of our time deciding, *Hmmm, should I get the Honey Nut Cheerios or the organic almond Kashi granola? Should I buy a boyfriend jean or a skinny jean? Should I watch HBO or TiVo?* Let's face it, we are in a capitalistically overwhelmed state. And this is no accident. While you're in the grocery store or the Gap deciding what to eat and what to wear, there are lobbyists and politicians in Washington passing bills that you know nothing about. They might be limiting your rights at the airport, in an abortion clinic, or at the gay pride parade. But you wouldn't know, because you're wondering whether your cereal has antioxidant powers or if that new pair of jeans will get you fucked.

Make no mistake. The government, the media, and commerce are actively collaborating to distract us from what's really important in life. After all, unconsciousness is a very effective commercial, political, and even military strategy. Keeping droves of citizens medicated and overstimulated with bullshit distractions pretty much guarantees that when they go to their polling places to vote, many will have no idea who the candidates on the ballot are, let alone what the propositions they're voting on say or mean.

Whoever said less is more was right: the less bullshit and frivolity you have in your life, the more attention you have to focus on what is *really* going on.

I want you to be able to see underneath, around, above, and through things, so that you can form and shape your own opinions, instead of just blindly going along with everyone else's. A good place to start is by understanding the media. I'm going to let you in on something: every media outlet is a *brand* with its own point of view. Writers who work at major international newspapers are asked to express themselves in a different way than tabloid reporters. Even my book is a brand! If I appeared in a pink tutu on my book cover, you'd probably find some other chick's book to read. As a publicist, I've spent twenty-five years learning the languages of different media brands. After all, if you're going to pitch a fashion story to an industry publication like *Women's Wear Daily* or Style.com, you may need a different slant than you would with *Life & Style Weekly* or *USA Today*. We like to say you have to frost the cake differently for different publications.

If you take a minute to actually look at these brands, from the major networks to the national newspapers, you'll see that many are owned by huge, multibillion-dollar corporations (that's billion with a *b*, baby!). Whether bringing you gossip or hard-hitting news, every brand is interested first and foremost in gaining more readers, viewers, or advertisers. Last time I checked, none of these major papers or networks had ".org" after their names; they are *for-profit businesses*. That means they have one responsibility to carry out for their owners and their boards: to engage you, the consumer or viewer, and keep you coming back for more.

How do they do this? At the top rungs of these networks and newspapers, you will find some of America's most talented college graduates. If you were to sit in on their creative meetings, you'd hear phrases like, "Wouldn't it be wild if we . . . ?" and "Can we try . . . ?" Many of these brands will try anything that works. I mean, let's be honest. How many times have you bought a tabloid promising that your favorite movie star couple was getting divorced or that some young starlet had suddenly sprouted cellulite?

GOOD EVENING, WELCOME TO THE NEWS: WHAT YOU'RE ABOUT TO SEE IS HIGHLY DISTURBING.

One of their favorite tactics is fear. Hundreds of producers employed by news organizations sit around every day scouring the Internet, reading every paper from coast to coast and every news feed from around the world. What are they looking for? Stories that are going to keep you hooked, scared, trusting them, and coming back for more updates, whether they're about Amish girls being slaughtered in their one-room schoolhouse by a milk truck driver in Pennsylvania, or the unspeakable home invasion tragedy of the Petit family in Connecticut, or the kidnapping of Elizabeth Smart. These were horrific acts perpetrated by psychopaths, but playing them over and over during the evening hours when most American families watch TV feels like an additional attack, both on the crimes' victims and on the rest of us.

I don't know about you, but this news is really freaking me out. And not just when I'm watching it either—it continues to haunt and stalk me afterwards. It's almost as if, after seeing the nonstop, sensationalized reporting of the Amish girls' story in 2006, my mind and heart opened a permanent portal through which I constantly revisit the scene of the crime, and I continue to pray for those girls and their families today. After being similarly besieged by coverage of the unspeakable tragedy of the rape and killing of three members of the Petit family in Connecticut, I could no longer just be at the mercy of these fears; I had to look at how they could be a teacher for me, and where I might actually be vulnerable. So I invested in a heavy-duty security system and started insisting on background checks for every person I hire at People's Revolution as well as independent contractors for my home. Only then did I start sleeping *even remotely* better.

You have probably already seen the warnings on various TV programs saying, "What you're about to see tonight is very disturbing." Well, I think these warnings are messages from the brands too—that you're about to get a big dose of your favorite drug, FEAR, delivered! Instead, I suggest a simple blue screen, perhaps counting down the numbers 3, 2, 1. And while we're at it, let's put blank covers on our newspapers, so that stories about young Disney stars "cutting" themselves and being diagnosed with borderline personality disorder don't menace our eight-year-olds when they pop into a bodega to get a candy bar on the way home from school. (I mean, can it really be a coincidence that the candy and newspapers are always stacked on top of each other?)

The people who work at media brands are experts at giving us not what we *want* to see, but what they know we won't be able to turn away from. They make it so that we can't help but look or click; they ensnare us with a combination of the Divine and the sadistic. In doing so, I believe they not only keep us numb and distract us from what's important in life—they manipulate us into wreaking more havoc on ourselves. After all, what we think is what we manifest, and I do not need or want people in the media helping me sculpt my thoughts.

Don't get me wrong, I love many members of the media, and I work with them all the time. (And my own industry has problems too; many designers put girls on the runway who look like carcasses.) But I'm tired of being terrorized by the "news." Over time, our perception and intention of ourselves and our lives can't help but become aligned with this fear-based messaging. It can make us paralyzed instead of proactive.

At the end of last year, I was reminded of the way some members of the media like to fuck our brains out with fear when, on the day after Christmas, the entire East Coast was hit with a blizzard. I mean, blizzards happen every year on the East Coast, but for some reason this one made front-page news in all the major papers and merited around-the-clock coverage by TV networks. To watch the news, you'd have thought that it was dangerous to even leave your house if you lived anywhere north of

Georgia! I happened to be down at my mom's in Virginia, and when I walked outside and looked around, I made the decision that—despite several states' governors having declared states of emergency, which was being eaten up by the media—I was from upstate New York, and I could handle this. I knew the Weather Channel was probably just thrilled about all the attention it was getting and blowing it way out of proportion, anyway.

I grabbed my daughter and got into my black SUV and we had a more than lovely drive, solo on the highway through several states. Sure, I went slow, but I made it to Baltimore in less than a day, driving mostly on black pavement. There, we checked into a four-star hotel and had a fabulous dinner. Meanwhile, Philly, one town over, was on near lockdown, as the Weather Channel continued to inform citizens of the dangers all around them. They bought water, firewood, and extra food. "The Eagles game will be cancelled! New York is totally shutting down!" You could practically see the local weather people wetting their pants with excitement. For them, this wasn't about protecting the citizens—it was their big moment! Their brand was blowing up!

It all reminded me of living in L.A. in my twenties, when on several occasions I was chilling at my friend's house on Mulholland, floating around in an inner tube in the pool with Joe Strummer from the Clash, when old acquaintances from New York would call me. "Are you okay?" they'd ask. "Have you seen the news? L.A. is on fire!" I'd say, "Really? Where?" And they would say, "Topanga!" which was eighteen miles away. Of course, the news stations would be carrying on as if the whole city was burning to the ground.

The truth is, it's a reporter's job to *report*; they have to report on news—or create it—to keep their jobs. National tragedies are not happening 24/7, but the news cycle is. As a publicist, I can tell you there's no one more receptive than a newsperson on a slow day. It's a gold rush: they need content! At the same time, you'd better hope Tom Cruise doesn't rescue a civilian in distress and that no one jumps off the Empire State Building on a day you're launching a press campaign or issuing a news statement, because you'll be fucked. It's the same reason you can't launch a new fashion label on Election Day. Sometimes you just can't compete.

Even the best news stories should just be a starting point, not the final word.

We can use them to pique our interest, but then we need to do our own research and create our own beliefs. There are too many capitalistic interests at work in the media—the media brands themselves plus the publicists and lobbyists whose job it is to influence them—to take any of it at face value. Everyone thinks news organizations exist just to inform us, but really they are distribution networks for branders, advertisers, and publicists, all of whom try to roll their ball down the lane and get a strike—that is, impact consumers. Think of the whole system like a big bowling alley, or better yet, an octopus whose tentacles are all intertwined.

As a publicist, it's my job to work with the media to get the word out about my clients' brands. Let me tell you how this works in the fashion world. If, for example, you're a publicist who has just taken on a new client—a hot young designer you want to blow up—you may start by making sure he or she is sold in the "right" five stores, because you know the fashion magazines will like this, and it will help you get a strike. Then, you'll want to "gift"—send the clothes completely free to—twenty or so really cool celebrities, editors, and stylists. Once those packages have been signed for, technically you can say that Miss Major Movie Star rocks your product.

Another useful tactic is to simply call the celebrity's manager or agent and throw down a money offer for the celebrity to wear the brand, whether exclusively through a three-, six-, nine-, or twelve-month contract or for a specific event like the Grammys, the Golden Globes, the MTV Music Video Awards, or the Oscars. This way you don't have to worry about celebrities dropping your brand at the last minute, because their publicist or friend from high school thought your competitor was cooler. It's a legal deal, babes. And this kind of thing has now has become its own industry: smart fashion brands look at *last year's* Oscar winners, who are sure to be this year's presenters, and make sure to get them on the payroll early! (This year's nominees aren't guaranteed to end up on stage, after all.)

Publicists are not the only ones using the media to get the word out about their brands. Government does it too. When the White House "leaks" information to the press, it's probably less a "leak" than a deliberate PR move. It's like sex tapes. I mean, do we really think *those* are accidents? Even citizens know how to use the media these days. Look at the "Balloon Boy" dad in Colorado! Every PR company in the country should have had its tail between its legs after that incident, because we're paid millions of dollars to get our clients on-air for fifteen minutes, and this country bumpkin from Colorado who wanted his own reality TV show managed to command the attention of news crews on both coasts for *forty-eight hours*!

It's really kind of easy. There are many ways to use and manipulate the news media to your or your brand's advantage, whether your brand is Gucci or the Obama administration.*

Unlike many of my competitors, I refuse to be a *normal* publicist. By that I mean I don't represent anyone or anything I don't believe in and genuinely enjoy being a mouthpiece for. At least, not anymore. When I first started People's Revolution, I had a business partner, and we never agreed on anything. I'd say Kartell; she'd say IKEA. She'd say the Grateful Dead; I'd say the Dead Kennedys. My partner screened clients by one criterion: If you have money, we'll take it. She felt that we weren't curators in a museum (I happened to disagree). My side of the room eventually came to include clients like the haute fashion designers Paco Rabanne and Vivienne Westwood, while she repped Hot Topic and a pornography company called the Adult Entertainment Network, a competitor to the infamous Vivid.

Back then, I was in the process of becoming bicoastal, as I represented an increasing number of New York–based fashion designers. I'd taken a small four-hundred-square-foot apartment on 47th Street between 9th and 10th Avenues, which is basically Times Square West. Every night, I'd hear pimps screaming at hookers outside my window. "What's my fucking name, bitch!" they'd yell. I'd hear lots of sobs as girls were physically and verbally abused. I started calling the police department to complain of the prostitution problem on my block, to no avail.

---

* In my opinion, Obama is the first president to actually kick ass with viral marketing and social media.

One day, my business partner asked me to cover a news interview for her. It was a media announcement being made by the head of the Adult Entertainment Network, an earnings report or an announcement on its growth. The interview was to take place in Times Square. So there I was, a few blocks from my house, with a very successful pornographer, facilitating his interview with a TV camera crew. Out of the corner of my eye I saw four police officers milling about the island in the middle of Times Square. I decided on the spot to reach out to them about the nagging prostitution problem on my block.

"Ma'am, are you some kind of wacko?" the officer asked, when I explained the problem. "You're standing in Times Square promoting pornography, and you're going to complain to me about the hookers on your block?"

He had a point. It was totally insane that I would simultaneously promote a porn network and complain about prostitution. Ultimately, I told my partner that it was the most humiliating professional experience I'd ever had and that I not only wanted nothing to do with the Adult Entertainment Network; I wanted it banished from our agency. (Of course, she told me to go fuck myself, and our partnership didn't last.)

Ever since then, I've taken on clients whose work I genuinely believe in, even if I wouldn't necessarily wear it myself. But unfortunately there are still plenty of very smart publicists and lobbyists out there whose entire job is to make you want shit that sucks or that's going to end up hurting or bankrupting you. Take candles (yes, even candles!). Most candles are made of paraffin, which releases carcinogens when it burns, meaning it has been linked to cancer by certain studies. Most candles also release more lead into the air than is safe, according to the Environmental Protection Agency (EPA). It's hard to believe, but it turns out that if you really want to kill your boyfriend, you should just cook him a really nice romantic dinner and light a bunch of candles! The most amazing part is that scientists have known about this since the 1970s. It's now forty years later! But candle companies don't want you to know about the research that exists out there on their products; nor do they want reporters to write about it, despite the fact that safer beeswax alternatives now exist. Instead, they want to seduce you with candlelight and beautiful smells. That's why they employ armies of publicists— to help spin the information you're getting.

Despite the fact that real information is more readily available than ever, we're receiving less and less of it, and we're able to actually understand even less than that.

I'M FUR-IOUS, AND I'M NOT FUCKING AROUND

Several years ago, I would've told you that you were out of your mind if you'd said I'd soon be working through the most significant recession my industry had ever seen, second only to the Great Depression. Left and right, magazines went out of business, boutique PR firms closed shop, and people went freelance or changed careers. But as the old media washed away, new ones rose in their stead. Hello, Facebook. Hello, Twitter. Both of these brands have become great assets for the public relations industry and for many people who want to find out what's really going on in the world. Prior to Facebook and Twitter, we had to pay $1000 to a service called PR Newswire to disseminate messages we wanted to send to multiple media outlets at once. Now, thanks to my multitiered platform—television and books—my company has the ability to reach over a hundred thousand people on Twitter, for free. I don't know about you, but I *love* having the ability to disseminate news straight to the people from my BlackBerry.

For example: I happen to think that, despite what industry insiders might tell you, it's absolutely gross that fashion people are still celebrating fur. What is so sexy about the annihilation of animals for clothing? I don't know what time period these people think we're living in. I feel the media have mistakenly portrayed fur as glamorous, when it is actually disgusting with a capital *D*. In fact, I was appalled when several prominent news organizations recently touted Naomi Campbell's hot sexy new fur campaign. Thanks to Twitter, I was able to instantly rebuff them by Tweeting that, if they think fur's sexy, they should show pictures of the animals being clubbed to death or perhaps with electrodes in their mouths or stuck up their anuses. (These are common practices to ensure the fur will lie perfectly on a coat.) *Then* we'll see how sexy it is. I was happy to know that a hundred thousand plus people read my message within minutes. And soon, hundreds of young people were even agreeing with me and *re*-Tweeting it.

I actually think that fur is a great lens through which to talk about commerce, publicity, fame, and the media—and how they all reinforce and rely on each other. Just like with political bills and Happy Meals (trust me, there is *nothing* happy about how that meal was made), the information about fur is already out there; everything relevant has been said. Take a minute out of your day to visit the website of People for the Ethical Treatment of Animals, PETA.org—I mean, just *one* minute, I beg you! View some videos of minks in their cages, suffering with open wounds and engaging in stress-induced cannibalism, or foxes with their legs stuck in traps, literally gnawing them off in terror. If you *still* think fur is sexy, then you should fucking take a ticket straight to hell and meet your other friends.

But denial is a dangerous drug. People have been programmed *not* to dig a little deeper to find out why they think something's sexy. In the comfortably numb generation, we think that seeing something on the news makes it true and that seeing something in the pages of our favorite fashion magazine makes it glamorous. And let's face it, fur's publicists have been doing a brilliant job for decades, selling fur to us via Davy Crockett, Dr. Zhivago, J. Lo, and other fur-wearing celebrities. (I'm literally on the Internet as I write this, trying to find a picture of someone who actually looks sexy in fur, but to me they all look like they're going to a screening of *The Flintstones*. If you want to look prehistorically ignorant, I recommend you run out and buy yourself a rabbit vest immediately.)

Often, fur trade associations befriend fashion designers when they're still in design school. They start by providing free fur, and later they pay them to use fur. Do you think I'm joking? I've literally had clients show pink mink gouchos in their summer collections. I'll ask them why they're doing this, only to find out they're being paid $10,000 by a fur company to use fur! (That's right, this shit is so ugly that its manufacturers have to *pay* to get it on the runway!) I hate to break it to you, but if you think fur's glamorous, it doesn't mean you have fabulous taste; it means you've been programmed to be totally numb to suffering.

Not that I blame you. I remember wanting a fur coat when I was growing up in Syracuse, in the Eskimo tundra of upstate New York. It always seemed like that's just what you wore to keep warm if you were rich and glamorous and that any good husband would eventually buy you one (of course, where I was from, even a rabbit stole was considered fancy). When I started representing fashion designers, I was given what I thought was a fabulous reversible flying fox coat by one of my clients. At the time, it was considered chic to bleach the fur and then dye the tips, so my coat was white with ombré hunter green accents. I wore it on a business trip to Sweden to visit a client; wrapped in it as I deplaned, I remember thinking how *in the game* I was. Never mind that Sweden is one of the most understated places on earth, and wearing a massive fur coat with ombré hunter green accents to Stockholm is like showing up in a Dior ball gown to a picnic. Despite wearing the only fur coat in the entire city, I still felt hot, not ridiculous.

I found out what's really going on in the fur industry from Dan Mathews, now vice president of PETA, whom I met early on in my time in New York. He visited me at Cutrone & Weinberg, my first PR firm, because he wanted me to know how fur was made. I thought he was a bit outlandish. After all, my impression of charities at the time was that they were supposed to be *nice*. PETA was attention-seeking and aggressive; at one point the organization even occupied the corporate headquarters of Calvin Klein until Calvin himself agreed to stop making furs.

But I didn't become antifur immediately. It took a few years for me to actually take ten minutes out of my busy day and spend some time looking into the industry. When I did, and when I saw some videos of what actually happens to these animals, I realized I could no longer get behind it. At first it was very personal; I just wouldn't wear fur myself. But as I later took my daughter shopping in stores that were selling turquoise fur vests to tweens, I realized I had a responsibility to use my platform to speak out against it. People in fashion, even if they disagree with the use of fur, do not speak out against it as a rule. They do not reveal their true opinions. To them I say, "Let's move on and be progressive. We don't need fur; it's outdated. What's more important, your outerwear or leaving your grandchildren a planet that's not violent and sadistic and out of harmony?"

I am not trying to be a Debbie Downer here. There is nothing wrong with owning nice things; everyone is entitled to bask in his or her good fortune, whether you're a publicist in SoHo or a middle-class kid in Syracuse shopping at the mall. But at the same time, we can't be drunk on faux glamour and frivolity. I am urging you to do your homework on *anything* you have been sold, whether a news story or a vest. We need to be able to see through the millions of brands vying for our attention in order to find out what we really need to know. I'm asking you, when you see something in the news or the media that you love or sparks your interest, to follow the story further. Think of it as a diving board into a beautiful lake: you need to jump off and swim across to get to the place you truly deserve to be. Ask questions, do some research, and develop your own point of view. Determine if both the end result *and* the origin are in line with what you believe in, instead of just blindly trusting and following everything you read or hear or see in the pages of your favorite magazine or newspaper. And don't be afraid if your opinion isn't the *normal* one—in fact, that probably just means you're on the right track.

I know it's sometimes easier to kick back than to think honestly about these things. I mean, sometimes *I* choose unconsciousness too. When I'm really in the mood for something, I can make myself forget about what's really happening, just like everyone else. Sometimes the want is just greater than the wince. But only when we start to dig deeper and understand the ways brands manipulate us can we make it stop. I'm not saying we're ever going to be doing our best in all areas, but we need to try to make our actions line up with our beliefs as much as we can. In doing so, we'll be shining a light down a long, dark hallway. Initially, these brands will try to ignore us. But if they want to stay in business, they're going to have to buckle and change. Look at *Super Size Me*, a documentary film about the health implications of eating Big Macs every day. Not only was it a huge embarrassment for McDonald's; it forced the company to start looking at changing its product offerings.

You, the almighty consumer, are the one that all these brands and their marketers, publicists, and reporters exist to sway. Everyone is trying to get your attention. They want your money and your devotion at any cost. And only you can put them out of business. Take a minute to figure out who you are in this equation and what you stand for. Then act accordingly.

And please, don't *ever* show up in fur to an interview at People's Revolution, because I will hang you upside down by Gravity Boots.

TWO

THE KELLA-SUTRA:
If You're Not Getting Fucked by Midnight, Go Home

One must shock the bourgeois.
—Baudelaire

Over the July 4th weekend last year, I stayed in New York to work. All my friends and frankly the whole city had skipped town, so on Saturday night I said to my daughter, Ava, "Grab your sweater and let's go out to dinner!"

"I'm sorry, Mommy," she replied. "I have other plans."

"You're eight! What plans could you possibly have?"

"I have to watch the new episode of *Hannah Montana*, followed by *The Suite Life*."

Bam—here it was, the downside to raising an independent child. Ava was literally the only person I knew in New York who was potentially available to grab a bite to eat that night, so once *she* blew me off, I was left to spend the evening by myself. Can you say "pathetic"?

I grabbed a few spiritual pamphlets, one called "Surrender" and one called "Grace," by my guru, The Mother, and walked to one of my favorite restaurants, on Mulberry Street. Unfortunately, while New Yorkers skip town on holiday weekends, the rest of the country—actually, many countries, including England, Italy, and France, the Navy, and the suburbs—descend. Little Italy was jam-packed. I settled into a corner table, the only New Yorker in the restaurant. I thought back to the first time I went to the movies alone, in the late 1980s. For about ten minutes I felt slightly odd and isolated, but then I realized I'm my own best company.

On this night, though, I was not allowed to enjoy my own company for long. Before even taking my drink order, my usual waiter approached to tell me that his teenage daughter had just gotten off work nearby and would love to meet me. Since I was alone, he wondered, could she sit at my table? "No" is actually one of my favorite words in the English language, but I couldn't manage to spit it out, since her father had always treated me well. With a sigh, I put down "Surrender."

She sat. She was a superfun, bubbly Italian American high-school girl, and she was on a mission. Her father was barely out of earshot when she launched an arsenal of questions.

"Can I ask you a few things?" she began.

"Sure," I replied, preparing to be grilled on whether she should wear an asymmetrical shoulder dress to prom or when she'd be too old to wear silly bands. Unfortunately, this wasn't what was on her mind.

"How do you give the perfect hand job?" she inquired.

Oh, Jesus.

OMFL.

I have to admit, my first instinct was to be flattered. Here I was, thirty years older than this girl and dining alone on a national holiday, yet she thought that I was still in the game—

that I had frontline information for her! Surely she wouldn't ask a seventy-five-year-old woman how to give a hand job. But I also knew I had to handle this carefully. I was in Little Italy, after all, and I didn't want to upset the girl's father, my waiter, since I'm sure he was "connected" (if you know what I mean). I'd come for pasta, and now I was just hoping to live through the night.

Still, I was intrigued. I started by asking the girl where she and her friends got their information about sex.

"We watch porn on the Internet," she replied.

"The Internet—*puh-leeeze*!" I gasped.

There *MUST* be something better!

I started to think about this. How tragic that we lavish money on our daughters' educations and on after-school activities from cheerleading and Chinese brush painting to field hockey and dance; we encourage them to excel academically and to find fulfilling careers; we send them to Paris and Israel to study culture; yet we spend *no* time or money teaching them how to have great, healthy adult sex lives. Instead, we merely mention menstruation and throw bras on them when they're thirteen. Or maybe we talk about the importance of birth control and tell them not to have sex. And then we never talk to them about it again.

There's just one problem: no one else is talking to them, either. Some girls will get lucky and have a sexually advanced classmate who can give them the information they're craving. But most others, like my new friend, are left foraging around in the dark.

Porn was the best we could do? I mean, don't get me wrong; is there anyone on the planet who hasn't watched it? I understand the curiosity, but I also believe there must be a higher way for young people to learn about sex. To be honest, porn can be more brutal than beatific. I'm not saying I think Ava is going to want to come to *me* for information on sex, even though I'd welcome any conversation with her. But I also don't want her to have to resort to watching a meth-addicted chick getting banged by some grandpa online. Where is the Vuitton bag of sexual teaching? Where is the elegance? Our sexuality is one of the most intimate and expressive aspects of ourselves; I'd never want my daughter to learn about it from someone I don't know and trust. What I want for my daughter is what I want for you: to have a safe, progressive, and expansive sexual life.

But before I gave this young woman in Little Italy any advice, I had to stop for a minute.

"Are you asking me this question because you want to extend your own sexual pleasure, or do you want to give your boyfriend a hand job to avoid having sex?" I asked.

She admitted it was "the last one." She didn't actually want to have sex until she was married—she just wanted to keep her boyfriend happy.

It saddened me that even at her age, trickery was taking precedence over technique. Although we hadn't taught this girl anything about sex, we *had* taught her how to be demure, coy, and shy—instead of just being honest. Maybe she did need to learn how to give the perfect hand job, but that was not what she was asking me. Lucky for her, I'm a good listener.

"I think you should put your own happiness first," I told her. "You should tell him you're not ready for this, and if he can't hang out with you through that, then you shouldn't be with him.

"The task at hand," I said, "is not learning how to give the perfect hand job. It's learning to speak up for yourself.*

"And as far as this part about saving yourself for marriage," I continued, "that is preposterous! You're not a bond or a stock. You *must* have sex before you get married, and lots of it."

Think about it. Would you ever buy a Bentley before taking it for a drive? Would you ever fly all the way to the Maldives without seeing a picture of your hotel? Then why would you marry a guy without being fucked by him? Sex is a superimportant part of a partnership, especially when the partners insist on monogamy by getting married. In an all or nothing world, you better dig the all, y'all!

Here's what I wish someone had told me when I was younger. We shouldn't just try to get by, in life *or* in sex. It's not enough. There's nothing worse than stroking a dick you don't care about. Nor should you ever go down on someone just because it's expected or to get him off your back. (Here's a tip: getting *on* your back doesn't get him off your back!) Sex is about much more than coming, even if most people do just fuck to come. It's not the end-all, be-all as porn and the movies might make you think. It's a *beginning*—a gateway to even greater things beyond your wildest dreams. Maybe you've already learned how to achieve an orgasm, a ten-second or ten-minute undulation of consciousness during which you're rippling and vibrating like the waves made by a stone thrown into a pond. But I hope you'll also learn

---

*This will also come in handy when you're married—"No, honey, not tonight!" is much better than a raw, nonpassionate hand job.

that you can extend that and make your love life a constant offering to the Divine—a state of ultraconsciousness.

When it comes to sex and making love, many women do not know how to express who they really are, or maybe they're just too intimidated to. Instead, they worry about whether they're giving a hand job the right way or having sex the right number of times per week. But the truth is,

Normal gets you nowhere, not even in sex!

The *normal* love life that most people are having in this country barely scratches the surface. We as women are accepting crumbs, when we should be feasting at the buffet.

That night in Little Italy, I had to apologize to my teenage friend, because my generation had failed her. I couldn't even think of a cool animated website to send her to to find the information she was looking for. In a flash, the marketer in me sprang into action, and I suggested she look into starting a new sex website with her friends. She'd surely make millions of dollars! Unfortunately, she didn't think that would fly so well with her family.

THE ONLY MISSILE I WANT TO SEE ON TV IS GOLD AND FITS IN MY MAKEUP BAG

It's beyond obvious that we need to start teaching our daughters sexual education and exploration in the same way and with the same tone that we teach them to read books or shop at luxury-brand stores. Unfortunately, we're still so uptight about sex in this country that when I recently arrived for an appearance on *Chelsea Lately* bearing a vibrator for Chelsea Handler, a totally modern chick, her producers informed me I was not allowed to show a vibrator on television. *Oh, really?* How interesting that we can show our children news footage of thousands of people being blown out of the windows of the World Trade Center in a mass murder over and over and over again or grainy footage from home-invasion videos, but we can't show them a missile-shaped gold object that exists purely to provide pleasure in the privacy of one's home (and that comes recommended by a slew of power chicks!). I believe our sexual repression is not just causing us to abandon our youth; it's helping make America the most dangerous place in the West to be a woman.

After that night in Little Italy, I started thinking about where I got my information about sex when I was growing up. Hmmm. From my dad's *Playboys*. My friends and I would steal magazines like *Playboy* and *Penthouse* from our parents and take them into our makeshift forts to pore over. We read Xaviera Hollander's "Call Me Madam" column in *Penthouse*, a soft-core section where "readers" would relay their sex fantasies. The best thing about stealing your parents' porn was that they couldn't come out and ask you for it. (I mean, really, "Did you steal our porn?") My dad probably went upstairs several times over the years to grab his *Playboy* for some private time, only to be foiled by my tribe of middle-schoolers sitting up in a fort in the backyard. One thing I remember about reading those columns was that they made sex seem fun, like this magical thing awaiting me in the future that was going to be really, really great. (I also remember that pearls were the hot accessory back then.)

Other than those *Playboys*, I rarely had the privilege of seeing anything that incited my fantasies when I was growing up. I definitely could have handled it if my mom had pulled out a few nipple clamps, an anal dilator, or even an electric vibrator, saying, "Listen, a lot of people believe that if you use an electric one, you'll burn out the nerves in your clitoris." Good to know! But she never did; nor did she advise me to read the great texts on lovemaking. Luckily, I've learned through experience. The journey of my life has been a continuous sexual education, from my first husband, a very accomplished lover seventeen years older than me (warning: once you have your first really great lover, it becomes as much a curse as a blessing, since successive lovers may not cut it) to my work with lingerie brands like Agent Provocateur, which, trust me, gave me in eight years an education in itself.

I hope your life will offer these lessons too. But I also encourage you to seek out information on sex, whether that means talking to a tribal council member or reading the *Kama Sutra,* an ancient Hindu text that is possibly the most famous book ever written about lovemaking. (One of the reasons I love India is that its culture makes room for everything in life to be included in the Divine—yes, even sex holds a sacred place! Contrast this to Mother Teresa, who ran around India for years telling people not to use condoms in the name of her religion, so that they could contract and die of AIDS instead.)

Or hey, how about this. Let's all write out our sexual fantasies. Most guys I've dated would have been beyond happy if I'd come up with a list of all the things I wanted to do and try with them. I mean, this is great third-date conversation material! I guarantee it'll get you a fourth date! Think about it. What guy wouldn't be happy if you said, "Hey, I really want to be tied up and blind-folded"? Obviously as you begin to explore, there will be certain things your partner wants that you'll object to, and if it's not your thing, feel free to speak up and say, "No, I will not pee on you!" But it's important to be carnivorous, spiritual, honest, and open.

When I was younger and just starting to have sexual experiences, I had thoughts and feelings I wanted to act on, but didn't. I was a Sicilian and a Scorpio, after all; I didn't want to scare anyone! It was only when I let go of society's and religion's ideas of what is right for me that I started to have better sexual relationships—and a *much* better time. Over the years I've had the great advantage of having certain lovers ask me, "What do you want?" And more often than not, they've wanted the same things. Guys are stumbling around in the dark too, so why not be each other's instructors? Everyone has a secret fantasy sex life. You might as well cop to it, find someone to share it with, and get it started.

As long as were on the subject of the *Kama Sutra*, well here's the *Kella-Sutra: A Guide to Stabbing Sexual Taboos*.

1. If you don't know yourself and what you want, then you have no business being in bed with someone else. Shakespeare said, "To thine own self be true." *If you aren't ready for it, don't do it.* Learn to speak up for yourself no matter who you're with or how old you are.

2. Do not be in places where you don't want to be, especially in states of intoxication.

3. The whole wait-two-days-before-you-call thing is a bunch of bullshit. Waiting in general is stupid; you have to be willing to reveal yourself, be vulnerable, and go for it, especially when the energy is there. They say that love is blind—this is true. Take advantage of that blindness, get on your cosmic rocket and fly into the violet outer space of your love! If there were really something to figure out, someone would have written a book called *The Rules,* and it would have *worked.* Love and relationships are as different as the two people who come together; each forms a combination the universe has never seen before. I'm not down with books like *He's Just Not That into You,* which teach chicks how to score a guy. Trust me, if a guy wants to put his dick in you, he will. There is nothing to figure out here!

4. If it's happening at the zoo, it could or should be happening for you. We can learn a lot about natural sexual behaviors by looking at our friends in the animal kingdom. Up to 75 percent of bonobos' sexual behavior is nonreproductive (these are the power girls of the animal kingdom). Male sea horses, long upheld as monogamous pillars of ocean society and thought to mate for life, were found in 2007 to be promiscuous, flighty, and more than a little bit gay (they also give birth to the babies). Two male lions have been observed fucking each other. Dolphins are known to pleasure themselves by rubbing against the ocean floor. To me, this says that things like homosexuality and masturbation are totally natural.

5. Do not pretend things are happening for you if they are not. Women are big orgasm fakers. I would venture a guess that 95 percent of the women reading this book don't even have real orgasms! We're programmed to tell a guy we're getting off even if we're not. You need to figure out your own body. If your hand didn't work, you'd go to a doctor for help in making it work, right? Well, your sexual health is no different. Experiment with vibrators and eroticism. Make appointments with yourself, so that you can start to get to know your body, since it's complicated. Seek out information from varied and trusted sources.

If you love someone enough, you can occasionally choose to offer up a shag without getting any result for yourself, but I don't recommend this as a ritual occurrence. The one thing you *can't* do is lie. You can't tell a guy he rocked you out or fake an orgasm to make him feel good. We don't tell people who can't carry a tune that they're great singers, so why would we encourage bad habits and abilities in bed? The good news, I can report, is that your body awakens even more after you have a baby; after I had Ava, I felt like a pinball machine that had only just been turned on. (But don't forget to ask for some extra stitches on your way out of the hospital to tighten your vagina and make future sex more pleasurable. Yeah, that's right, your mom's probably not going to tell you *that* either.)

6. Take no prisoners; and if you do, make sure you untie them in the morning, so they can go to work and make money. (And vice versa. I mean, let's face it; there's nothing worse than having to call in with the truth: "I'm late today because I'm all tied up here at home!")

7. Lovemaking does not always have to involve a penis and a vagina (or two penises or two vaginas). Perhaps it means you rub my feet for two hours, and we feed each other. A four-hour lovemaking session isn't necessarily what I want when I've worked around the clock in three cities all week. Learn to be sensual, not just sexual. It's said that Mary Magdalene washed Jesus's feet with her hair. Imagine waking up and loving a man so much that you literally express your love and adoration by patiently braiding his hair in floral essences. Alternatively, you could try wearing matching pajamas and eating Orville Redenbacher popcorn on the couch under a blanket while you watch your favorite TV show. These types of offerings can be beautiful and should be booked in your love calendar. (Yes, I believe we need to book our sex rituals with each other the same way we book meetings.)

Bathing, combing each other's hair, reading favorite childhood stories to each other—there are plenty of ways to be sexy. A lot of married people I know don't even know about tantra, a practice in which the male doesn't come, because he wants to hold the sexual energy in his body rather than let it flow out of him. (Translation: if you're involved in a tantric relationship, you'll have sex for at least ten hours, but in those ten hours you might stop to have some sherbet or check your e-mail. This is a proper day of lovemaking.)

8. If you're not getting fucked by midnight, go home. Recently, one of my friends was in Paris producing fashion shows when she met a famous French deejay. Apparently they really hit it off, because he told her he'd be coming to New York in a few weeks and asked if he could stay with her. Excited, she agreed. She didn't realize that she'd soon be in the process of changing apartments. So she booked a hotel room for herself and the deejay.

I don't know about you, but if I'm invited to stay in a guy's hotel room for more than three days and he's footing the bill, I infer that sex will probably be in the mix, unless he's a relative or religious figure. (As I said before, if you don't want to be in a situation like this, *leave.*) But after three or four days of total confusion, my friend called to tell me it wasn't happening with the French deejay. I immediately told her she needed to throw down and be honest. "Tell him, 'If we are not going to have a sexual relationship, or at least an emotional relationship that's going to lead to a sexual relationship, then you need to leave, because your Frenchness is bumming me out.'"

When I returned to my office the next morning, my friend was there, hanging out with one of my publicists, still shocked and devastated by this guy's behavior. "I want you to go in my office," I said. "Find those photos of me when I was your age, the ones that no longer look like me. I want you to know that even when I looked like *that*, I thought I was defective—that I was the problem! You have to accept the fact that if this were meant to be, he would have jumped on top of you long ago."

The point is, we can put these situations on Freud, or we can put them on cultural differences, but we should *not* put them on our hotel bill.

9. If you're sleeping with a married man, you're *helping* him stay married. A married man will never leave his wife for you. If you had asked me twenty years ago whether men or women end most relationships, I definitely would have said, "Men." And in my two marriages I spent a lot of time wondering whether I was keeping my husband happy enough. But I now have enough life experience to know that when a man finally commits to a chick, he may eventually cheat on her with her best friend or drive her crazy eating Doritos on the couch all day like a sack of potatoes, but he is *never* leaving, regardless of how much he can't stand her. He will always make her lower the boom. And even then she probably won't be able to get rid of him! I mean, Spencer Tracy wouldn't leave his wife for the great Katherine Hepburn, despite the fact that they spent thirty years together and costarred in nine films!

Years ago, after my first husband, Ronnie, made me kick him out,* I met a really beautiful German rock star, who was in the INXS of Germany. I could hardly believe my good luck. He was blonde, funny, great in bed and had the hottest south German accent I'd ever heard. To top it all off, he lived at the Chelsea Hotel. I mean, can you say *Traum*, baby? Within two weeks, we'd embarked on a massive love affair. We traveled together and hung out with each other's friends, and every night after working in the studio, where he was recording an album with my musician friend, he appeared at my apartment on Hudson Street in the West Village.

One day about a month into our relationship, I ran into a friend of mine named Nico, who always knew everyone's business. Nico mentioned that he'd heard I was dating this German rock star and wondered if I knew he had a three-month-old baby at home in Germany, *with his live-in girlfriend*. I felt as though I'd

---

* His strategy was to sit around watching the Yankees all day and talking about the apocalypse, while wearing an oversized nightshirt that said, "Shut up and go to sleep." It worked.

been hit in the head with a ton of bricks while being kangaroo-kicked in the heart. There was just no way. Nobody could fuck me so hard and so pure and be so corrupt at the same time.

"It can't be the same guy," I said, shaking my head. I was about to learn that men have an amazing ability to compartmentalize. (FYI, so do women, but we're not talking about us right now.)

"Why don't you ask him?" Nico suggested gently, almost daring me.

That night, when the rock star knocked on the door, I opened it only halfway.

"Hey, babe," he said.

"Before you come in, I have a question for you," I said accusingly. "Do you have a girlfriend? Better yet, do you have a *baby*?"

He nodded. "Yeah," he replied, with a slight tinge of annoyance that said, *How inconvenient you're finding out about this in the middle of our wild love affair.*

That's when I swung my fist and punched him harder than I've ever hit anyone in my life. Then I slammed the door in his face.

Outside, he banged and pleaded in vain. "Come on, we need to talk about this," he said.

I just sank to the floor and cried and cried, vowing never to speak to him again.

The truth of the matter is, you just never know what's going on with people. I believe that even if a guy tells you he's separated, divorced, or about to get a divorce, it doesn't hurt to do a little digging around on the Internet or even pay a few bucks for a background check. I mean, there are just so many different family systems out there today. It's not enough to just ask if he's married;

you may need to come up with five or six ways to find out whether he's in a relationship! Does he live with another human being besides his child? Is he in *any* sort of ongoing sexual relationship with someone to whom he is not related?

I've actually been forced to learn this lesson more than once. Five years ago, I'd become an eco-dater, meaning I was only sleeping with people I'd already slept with in the past. It was around then that I reconnected with my ex-boyfriend Jimmy, whom I'd dated on and off since 1991. We'd both had kids with other people, but he told me he was no longer intimate with his son's mother, with whom he was still living "platonically" in L.A. And guess what? I fucking believed him! That's right, at thirty-five years old, ten years after my affair with the German rock star, *I believed him!*

Several months into our bicoastal relationship, I flew out to California to shoot an ad campaign. When I invited Jimmy to come, he told me to pick him up on the corner of his street. (Here's a tip: don't ever agree to pick anyone up on the corner.) As I drove up, my phone rang. *"Hit the pedal!"* he screamed. "Don't stop driving! Go, go, go!"

Before I knew it, I was being chased down Wilshire Boulevard by a silver soccer-mom Volvo station wagon. *Oh fuck,* I thought. *It's Jimmy's wife.* (Here's another tip, sisters: a married woman who is not sleeping with her husband *will not chase her husband's lover down Wilshire Boulevard at ninety miles an hour in her silver hatchback soccer-mom Volvo.* Translation: wife is still sleeping with husband, boyfriend is a liar, and you are in danger.)

I stomped on the pedal of my rented SUV and tore off with the Volvo hot on my tail, weaving through traffic, trying to make a right turn while keeping my speed up. Eventually I lost her, which is when I had to admit Jimmy's behavior was affecting my work. I was now late to my shoot. Fuck him!

If you have the bad luck of entering a relationship with someone who's still in the process of leaving his last one (or hasn't yet), I suggest you put on your listening ears. He will probably try to tell you his ex-wife or girlfriend is crazy or, better yet, hysterical, a word that is derived from a term meaning "in the uterus," and go on to describe her faults. What he's actually about to give you is a list of everything that's wrong with *him*. It may sound at first as though the woman is in fact out of her mind, but there's a good chance a lot of the problems she's complaining about are the ones you're about to inherit.

When my first ex-husband's fourth wife—did you get that?—called me years after my divorce to complain about him, I was antiquing in southern Virginia with my daughter. It had been years since I'd been married to Ronnie—I was now a happily single mother—but hearing this woman talk about him made me feel as though my divorce had been yesterday. "He won't let me take his car; he's saying I should have thought to get my own tires changed. He looks like the Wolfman. He's chasing me around saying he's going to kill me!" she moaned. I mean, it was basically a play-by-play reenactment of my own breakup with my husband! Yes, Virginia, history and our lovers' bad behaviors tend to repeat themselves.

It was just this past year, while working on this book, that I told Ava's father, an Italian, the story of the German rock star and me, and how I confronted him on that fateful night. Ilario started laughing in his beautiful Italian accent.

NORMAL GETS YOU NOWHERE

"That's funny," he said. "That's the difference between an Italian and a German man. A German man will tell you, 'Yes, there is a baby,'" he said. "An Italian man will say, 'Baby? What baby?'"

10. Just because you're great lovers doesn't mean you're going to live happily ever after. News flash: there is a huge difference between being great lovers and being partners. Just because a guy can throw down and fuck your brains out does *not* mean you're going to be able to grocery shop together and get your bills paid. Yes, sex is superimportant, but it's a small part of partnering. We shouldn't call someone our partner or even our boyfriend if they're really just our lover. Sometimes in life, you'll have a lover who is not meant to be a partner. And sometimes it's okay to just enjoy having a lover for a few years. We need to figure out the reasons we want a relationship, anyway. In some cases, we just want someone to baby-sit us, because we don't want to be alone with ourselves.

This was the case when I married my second husband, Jeff. I had just been signed to a deal with Atlantic Records at the time, meaning I had a lot of time on my hands (I mean, what was I supposed to do all day? It only took me a few minutes to write a song!) and very little money, a lethal combination. It wasn't long before I'd ditched the record deal and started my own company, though, while my husband remained a struggling actor. He'd always say things like, "We're partners, baby."

Oh really? I'd wonder. How exactly are we partners? You're doing exactly what you want, which is working on your acting career, which generates no money for this house, while I'm earning cash, going to the

grocery store, cooking the food, and doing all the other things that have
been considered feminine responsibilities for thousands of years, only to
be told I'm escalating and need some rest!

I know from friends that if you're going to attempt to be the breadwinner in the relationship, you're going to need some regular checks and balances. It doesn't have to be about male/female; it can just be about person/person. Who is doing what, and how is each partner contributing to the overall relationship? Is one person feeling like shit? Does one feel like the other's friends think he's a loser? Jeff never wanted to go to any of my work events, because he said no one wanted to talk to him. Which was ironic, since for decades women have been showing up to work events of their husbands *assuming* that no one wanted to hear what they had to say—that they were just there to look good in a dress.

You can't have a real partnership without dialogue. Few people pause to consider whether they're actually compatible with someone before starting a relationship; they just start getting fucked and think, *Oh my God, this is it!* But real partnership is about much more than great sex: Do you have the same desires for your lives? Where do you want to live? What do you want your life to look like? What happens if you're the one making money? Does the other still expect you to go to the grocery store too? This isn't rocket science. We need to deprogram ourselves from thousands of years of stereotypes, but at the same time we can't kid ourselves about who we really are. If what you really want is to make money and have a career, you probably aren't going to be the one cooking dinner every night. That's where a partnership can be valuable, if you do it right.

LOVE IS A CRAZY-ASS BLINDFOLDED ANGEL WITH A WEAPON IN HIS HAND

Just after I had my daughter, a handsome lawyer I'd drunkenly made out with one night in the early 1990s started positioning himself to be my next boyfriend. He even sent Ava her first Christmas snowsuit. My mother could hardly believe my good fortune. Here I was, parenting a little one-year-old girl all by myself, and I had an Italian American lawyer from upstate New York—a mere fifteen miles from where I was born—lining up to marry me! He was basically my mother's ideal son-in-law. I was forced to deliver the crushing news that, although this lawyer was amazing, cute, and all-around great, there was just one problem: I didn't have energy with him. I didn't want to kiss him, and I most certainly did not want to fuck him.

This is when my mom decided to do a reenactment of 1640 and insisted that "that part will come in time." The fact that people went to bed by candlelight the last time anyone actually believed such nonsense didn't seem to give her pause. I mean, I'm now forty-five, and I've still yet to meet *one person* who was initially turned off by her husband, but found herself fucking him like a rabbit seven years into their marriage. This is why, although the lawyer continues to be a friend of mine and I will always appreciate that he showed up to be my suitor, he now has a Russian model for his wife.

Let's be honest. Most of the time when we fall in love with someone, it's not because the wider world has given us any indication that their dick should be inside of us. *Energy* has nothing to do with what's practical or aesthetic; it has nothing to do with his stats, his bank account, or how he looks on paper. It is not the same as *attracted to* or *makes sense*. Instead, it comes directly from the source. Most of the time when you meet someone, you're either in or you're out. Does he make you want to do crazy things? If he doesn't, and you're just trying to figure out how to keep him happy or how to leave by noon the next day, you're a *liar*, not a lover, and I'm sorry to be the one to tell you that if you continue this relationship, you're going to need a lawyer.

One of the great things about making my own money is that I've always been able to fuck who I wanted, not who I thought would marry me or take me shopping. Maybe it's not good to keep bringing my daughter into the sex chapter, but I recently gave Ava her own wallet, allowance, and cash card. She's eight; I thought it would be a good way to teach her math. After Ava made her first purchase (clothes at a store called Justice), calculating what she could afford, then counting the money out carefully, and handing it to the clerk, she was thrilled. "You know what was really good, Mommy?" she said afterwards. "I didn't have to say thank you to anybody."

I believe that's how our love lives should be too. We should be with someone because we truly love them, and our soul wants us to be with them, not because they're going to buy us a great apartment or Birkin bag. Can you even imagine having to sleep with some of those businessmen who look like they've been stranded in an English library since 1820? I mean, maybe some of them are smart and interesting, but I've seen plenty a girl out in the Hamptons who looks like she can't wait to see her tennis instructor.

When I was younger, I passed up a possible opportunity for an assignation with Leonard Cohen, one of my favorite musicians. I was signed to Atlantic Records at the time, and one of my employees had played my album for his daughter. He'd heard my music and invited me out for coffee. I didn't go, because I was married, and I knew I didn't want to get coffee with Leonard; I wanted to fuck him. I mean, he is *ridiculous*! To this day, Leonard's song "Hallelujah"—which has been covered by about 150 other artists, including Jeff Buckley—contains one of my favorite lines about sex, or at least how sex *should* be: "Remember when I moved in you / The holy dove was moving too / And every breath we drew was Hallelujah."

If you have ever had the great privilege of crying when you make love with someone, then you will understand what it's like to be a god, an angel, and a human being all at the same time. I have at certain times in my life cried while making love, and in those moments I've been delivered with my lover to places we didn't know we were capable of going. We got there with energy and gentleness and roughness and a deep mutual respect, but most of all through vulnerability and self-revelation. Through total transparency of expression, we achieved the great cry and the great exhaustion and the great nothingness of all that is. This is what it means to make love, I think. (Hey babe, I'm doing my best here. I'm sure not everyone wants sex tips from Mama Wolf, but someone needs to be talking to you about these things!) As beings, we should insist on this. Should you have the great privilege of being with a partner who can embrace you through your tears as you mutually strengthen one another—well, *that* is a great relationship.

The truth is, when you do it right, sex is not all that different from church. Yes, that's right. Falling to your knees to pray and asking God to help you is not *that* different from lying on your back with your legs spread, saying, "I love you. I want to taste the nectar of Divine consciousness through you." We're just small human beings, after all, and physical love allows us to dance a special magical dance that is both part of our destiny and larger than ourselves.

The world is a dangerous place. When we make love, we're acknowledging, *Yes, even my family doesn't really know me. So I, this strange swan in this big, strange pond,* choose to hook up to you and allow you to be inside of my body. I trust you, and I'm transparent, and through this vulnerability and mutual sense of adventure your consciousness and my consciousness will intertwine like strands of DNA to create a song of magic and sensory heightening that is one of the closest things to God and the Goddess on this earth.* This oneness is an offering—an acknowledgment and expression of the Divine's magic. And trust me, it has rarely been adequately captured in sex drugs, rock 'n' roll, film, or fashion.

When you explore sex and love with someone, you're agreeing to enter into a new type of yogic teaching—one in which you have a lot to give *and* a lot to learn (it's like having a child). I promise that you will hate your lover sometimes. You'll also laugh with each other, cry with each other, fuck each other, and fuck each other over. Being truly yogic with another means offering

---

* I've put on swan costumes occasionally in my life, but the Divine always poofs me back into a wolf or an eagle!

up your whole self, just like you do when you pray in church. And let me tell you, making love with someone you love is a much more powerful thing than sitting in a church that doesn't let women speak. You're basically saying, *This is our love, our song, our vibration of love and ecstasy that we send out into the universe.* Making love, like making war, creates a powerful and totally unique vibration.

A warring lovemaking session—now that's a fucking *great* vibration!

THREE

HOLY DAZE
(HOLLA, DAYS OFF!)

Illegal aliens have always been a problem
in the United States. Ask any Indian.
—Robert Orben

Years ago, in my twenties, when I was reading tarot cards on the beach in Venice for a living, I was hearing a lot about the end of the world. I remember thinking about what it would be like to experience the apocalypse. One year, it occurred to me that I already was experiencing the apocalypse, and that it was Christmas! You know, the holiday where everyone runs around buying ridiculous and unneeded gifts for $19.99 in the name of their God as they trip over homeless people on the street wearing signs like "Hungry. Please help" and ignore Santas ringing bells for the Salvation Army. I mean, wouldn't it be wonderful if there really *was* an army for salvation? Instead, there's just one big long line outside the UGG store.

When my daughter was born, I was adamant that I did not want to bring her up with lies. I was willing to celebrate Christmas and even have a tree, but I wanted to tell her that Santa represents the spirit of giving, *not* that he was literally someone who lived at the North Pole and brought presents to kids. Similarly,

I'd tell her the Easter Bunny represented spring. As for the Tooth Fairy, well, she's such a great creation that I figured I'd just give in and go along with that one. (I mean, whose idea was it to make having a tooth fall out in the middle of the day something to get *excited* about?)

So I told my mother I was not going to do the whole North Pole, Santa thing with Ava. I mean, we spend so much time and money getting our kids all wound up about Santa and the Easter Bunny, making them think these fake apparitions are going to appear and make life magical, when everyday human kindness can really do the same thing.

"Are you *crazy*?" my mom said. As soon as Ava could hold the phone to her ear, my mom could barely wait to shriek, "Santa Claus is married to Mrs. Claus, and they live at the North Pole, and their reindeer are Dasher and Dancer and Prancer and Vixen, Comet and Cupid and Donner and Blitzen! And the elves make all the presents! Santa's very modern now, you can e-mail him!" Last year she even topped herself, convinced this would be one of the last years when Ava would believe in Santa. She literally bought Ava a copy of *The Night Before Christmas* that came with a voice recorder into which she'd programmed herself reading the text aloud. Ava is a pre-tween at this point, and my mom's still trying to give her one last hit of Christ-mess!

Why have we all been suckered into celebrating a holiday that very few of us actually believe in?

Wouldn't it be great if we all just decided we didn't want to do Christmas one year? What if, instead, we found things that *do* matter to us to celebrate, or at the very least just took a really great vacation? I want to go on record as saying that if you have children, Christmas is possibly something you should do. And don't get me wrong; there must be a few Christians out there who actually believe Christmas is Jesus's birthday, and by all means they too should celebrate it. If Christ is your guru, throw him a party and get down with it. But he's not my guru, and I resent the fact that I'm still supposed to spend $8,000 on presents for everyone I know each December, including vendors, business acquaintances, and my trainer. There's so much pressure to buy gifts and plane tickets and go home to our families and be intimate, but then we do, and no one even talks about real things or has real conversations! I mean, even Jewish families are being pressured by the Christmas complex; they're buying blue Hanukah bushes at Target, because their kids feel bad Santa's not coming to see *them*!

We don't *have* to go along with this. Remember, normal gets you nowhere—you don't have to celebrate the normal holidays, especially when they get you stuck in an airport on December 23 with a bunch of angry, violent people. Why not make your own holidays, just as I've urged you to make your own religion? Merriam-Webster defines "holiday" as "a day on which one is exempt from work; specifically, a day marked by a general suspension of work in commemoration of an event." I hate to tell you this, but as a single mother I spend the Christmas "holiday" running around like Mrs. Brady on crack. I get off work at nine or ten at night, fly up to Times Square in a cab, work my way through Toys 'R Us, then try in vain to cram my bags into another cab in the freezing cold before giving up and opting for delivery.

I mean, there's nothing restful about it. Frankly, anyone who tells you it's restful is either lying or on meds.

Instead of these fake holidays commemorating things that didn't even happen (Most scholars don't even think Jesus's actual birthday was in December!), I propose all employers give their employees at least five to ten personal days per year in addition to their sick and vacation days. This way, we could take a day off work anytime we think something is holy. If you want your self-made holiday to be January 5—which I highly recommend, since travel is cheaper than ever and everything's 50 to 90 percent off—then go for it! If you'd rather celebrate the Navajo Sing Festival in February or the Hindu Ganesh Chaturthi festival in September, go for it! People who aren't religious could vacation à la France, combining all these days into a month off in August. Alternatively, they could just stay at the office on the traditional holidays and get paid time and a half while everyone else goes home to celebrate their holidays!

Let's be honest. Presidents' Day? Is there one American who actually spends this day celebrating our presidents? Columbus Day? Do we really need a mandatory day off to celebrate one of the most destructive humans in history? No one's sitting home reading about Columbus on that day, anyway, so why not just eliminate it? Mother's Day is actually the only current American holiday I can really get behind, provided we combine it with Father's Day to turn it into Parents' Day, so that kids who only have one parent or two same-sex parents don't feel bad. I mean, why should I be forced to take a day off on Columbus Day instead of on my own guru's birthday, February 21? Leonard Cohen's birthday would also be a holiday in my church. I'd probably also take a yearly holiday to Amsterdam with a few girlfriends to celebrate our friendship and our love for each other. Doesn't this all make much more sense? What matters to you, and what would *you* celebrate?

DUDE, YOU'RE TALKING TURKEY

Thanksgiving is one of my least favorite American holidays. Like Christmas, it has become a huge industry. Each year, we celebrate it by slaughtering 45 million turkeys and eating (on average) 4,500 calories in a single meal. There's just one problem. What are we celebrating? I didn't figure out that Thanksgiving was a totally fabricated holiday until I met the American Indian leader John Trudell—who became my lover, teacher, and lifelong friend—in 1991. That's when I started thinking honestly about the fact that every year, hundreds of millions of Americans sit around and eat turkeys to celebrate our annihilation of an entire race of people.

All throughout school, I'd been taught in history class that Thanksgiving was to commemorate the pilgrims and the Indians shaking hands, making friends, and eating corn and squash for dinner. But what really happened is that Europeans came over and obliterated this continent's inhabitants with guns and diseases and then stole their land. The ones they couldn't kill off, even after hundreds of years of wars, they crowded onto the worst tracts of land—Indian reservations—and plied with cigarettes and alcohol. Over the years, the "Americans" told the Indians to give up their spiritual practices, from medicine wheels to Sun dancing, to cut their hair, change their names, and learn English if they wanted to continue to receive subsidies.

This is what we celebrate when we celebrate Thanksgiving. In many schools, we're still brainwashing our children with these lies. Can you imagine what the Indian kids must be thinking? It would be like everyone in New York City having cake for Hitler's birthday! I don't understand why there aren't twenty-five thousand Indians outside Macy's each year protesting this! Where is everyone? Are they all on the Internet?

Despite the fact that the first alleged "Thanksgiving" happened in 1621, it wasn't until 1939 that Thanksgiving became the caloric binge it is today. That's when President Franklin Delano Roosevelt officially proposed that it happen annually on the last Thursday of November—not in order to celebrate history or our heritage (even lies about our heritage), but *to extend the Christmas shopping season and stimulate the economy*! In 1941, Congress took Roosevelt's lead and gave us all the day off. Yes, that's right. This holiday is fewer than a hundred years old, which means it can still be stopped!

Don't get me wrong. No one loves black and white together more than I; in fact, dozens of designers have done amazing interpretations of the buckle shoe already. And Black Friday—please. I know it's a huge day for my industry and has helped pay my bills by bolstering my clients' businesses. I have nothing against holidays or celebrating; I just don't know why we'd want to celebrate a holiday with no meaning that makes us strung out, fat, and broke.

And I resent the fact that, when I go to my local farmer's market on weekends in November, I have to see a poor turkey in a cage under a sign that says, "Order Here," and be forced to explain to my daughter that this beautiful creature, which Benjamin Franklin wanted to name our national bird, is about to be slaughtered and eaten. Humans have celebrated the solstice and the changing of the seasons for thousands of years. Why can't we just say we're taking a time-out for four days to each celebrate what we want, with a smile on our face and a prayer and a song in our heart?

When I first found out the truth about Thanksgiving, I fasted on that day, refusing to justify this fake, violent holiday with my participation. After a few years, I decided it would be more productive to make it into my *own* holiday. So I started throwing a "harvest dinner," inviting a handful of friends and sometimes employees to my apartment, where we'd cook root vegetables and celebrate the harvest, the changing of the seasons, and everything in our lives we have to be grateful for. We don't need a fake historical event to justify this—and I can assure you we are not missing out on anything.

When you really start to look at our modern holidays, you'll see they have almost nothing to do with history, religion, or tradition and everything to do with capitalism—which wants to keep us acting "normal," or distracted from what's real and numbly consuming as much stuff as possible. Until the 1980s, most stores were closed on holidays like Presidents' Day. But these holidays have become huge boons to retail; stores stay open to capitalize on the fact that the government has given us all a mandatory day off when we're free to shop! Presidents' Day now is best known not for presidents, but for car discounts. Yes, it has become one of the biggest car-buying days of the year! Valentine's Day, meanwhile, is a huge day for the chocolate, flower-delivery, and restaurant businesses. I mean, entire industries revolve around these supposedly restful "holidays."

Meanwhile, Anna Jarvis, the West Virginian who invented Mother's Day and got President Woodrow Wilson to approve it in 1914, was arrested later in her life for protesting the commercialization of this holiday she helped create! Yes, she gets *one* holiday celebrating women on our whole fucking calendar, only to be disgusted when it's taken over by capitalism. Jarvis even opposed selling flowers and greeting cards, calling them "a poor excuse for the letter you are too lazy to write."

Please, will you join me in putting these holidays out of business?

Let's celebrate the things *we* want to celebrate by creating our own personal holidays and traditions, making them restful, meaningful, and yes, even spiritual.

And let's stop shopping on days when the government and capitalism tell us to and instead shop when everything's on sale!

FOUR

AWAKENING UNIVERSAL MOTHERHOOD:
My Three-Way with Wonder Woman, Eleanor Roosevelt, and Amma

I have spent many years of my life in opposition,
and I rather like the role.

Do what you feel in your heart to be right—for you'll
be criticized anyway. You'll be damned if you do, and
damned if you don't.

—Eleanor Roosevelt

PART I: ULTIMATELY, THERE'S NO SUCH THING AS COINCIDENCE OR BAD PUBLICITY

One day last summer, I received a phone call from the *New York Post* informing me that DC Comics had created a new look for Wonder Woman and asking for my opinion. *What?* I thought. *Why would they change her look? She looks amazing!* I happen to think Wonder Woman's look is one of the few things in the world that *shouldn't* change. After all, there's really nothing like a hot chick in star-spangled briefs, knee-high boots, arm cuffs, and a red and gold corset with a lasso and supernatural powers. Who doesn't love that?

I hadn't seen the new look yet, so I pulled it up on the Internet. I was disappointed, to say the least. This was surely a fashion "don't." As in, *don't* take a really hot superhero known for saving lives in a Thierry Mugler-esque getup and reduce her to jeggings and a cropped bolero. It was pathetic! Besides, we were in the middle of a recession. How had no one thought to call some American designers to ask them to redesign her look? That would have been a good PR strategy! I told the *Post* exactly what I thought, and then later I vlogged about it on "Wake Up and Get Real," the internet talk show I do with my best friend Justine Bateman. Wanting my comments to be alliterative, I said that Wonder Woman had gone "from Paris to Poughkeepsie." (I consider myself something of an aficionado of mall looks in Poughkeepsie, since I spend many a Sunday strolling the Poughkeepsie Galleria near my weekend home.)

It wasn't long after the *New York Post* piece and my vlog appeared that I started receiving calls from a guy named John W. Barry, a reporter for the *Poughkeepsie Journal*. At first I didn't call him back. I didn't have to be psychic to figure out he was probably calling with a feather up his ass over my comment, and I was not in the mood to defend myself over such a lame topic or to let some reporter turn me into a big Poughkeepsie hater. Especially when Poughkeepsie is a place I've been very connected to for years. I mean, I spend a ton of cash at the Target there every weekend. I let my love *flow*! Would I really be in the process of buying my first home just a few minutes from the town if I hated it so much?

But after his fifth phone call, I thought, *Oh God, I'll just throw him a bone and be nice.* Unfortunately, talking to him was a bit of a joke. My initial feelings were confirmed; he had prepared a list of journalistically prodding questions and kept pelting me with them over and over in hopes that I'd break down and admit I actually did hate the town, which in fact was simply not true. I hurried off the phone.

The next day, driving up to my country house, I stopped at my usual gas station. The attendant, who looks like a Bangladeshi Clark Kent and whom I've seen every weekend for the past eight years, seemed especially excited to see me.

"Ohhhh, you're on the cover of the paper!" he said.

Oh fuck.

In that moment, I got what it must be like when you've robbed a bank and you're trying to quietly skip town. There I was, standing at the counter with two pink Snowball cupcakes that looked like big nipples, reaching for a loaf of white Wonder Bread— yes, it's the only thing Ava will eat her grilled cheese on—while Clark Kent waved a copy of the *Poughkeepsie Journal* at me with large pictures of my face and Wonder Woman's on it. "'Wonder' Blunder? Jab at Poughkeepsie About Comic Icon's New Look Draws Notice," blared the headline. The article inside noted: "Comments about Wonder Woman's makeover have residents wondering why Poughkeepsie was the apparent target of a fashion publicist." I'll tell you why: it was a slow news day in upstate New York!

I know people say there's no such thing as bad publicity, but in the moment it can feel pretty bad. After all, I'd been a good sport with the *New York Post,* and the piece turned out to be quite a bit of fun. But for me, it quickly turned to sour apples when I saw myself on the cover of the *Poughkeepsie Journal.* It had been years since I'd thought about Wonder Woman. Yet while others were talking about the recession, depression, national debt, and fear and violence, I was talking about hot pants. That was my big contribution to a cover story. *What is my life coming to?*

I wondered. To be honest, the whole thing made me feel kind of chippy.

Luckily, sometimes what seems at first like an annoyance, a setback, or a really huge mistake can actually be part of something much larger. I've told you many times that I do not believe in coincidences. I do believe every moment is engineered by our soul and the Divine. In fact, some experiences, both good and bad, are meant to teach us what we need to know at a certain time. Look at it this way: Our soul and the Divine are conductors in the rock opera of our lives, and though I didn't know it at the time, the summer of 2010 would be, for me, a song with a great motherfucking hook. Can you believe that Cutrone's cutting comments (there I go with the alliteration again) about Poughkeepsie would lead to an invitation to visit Eleanor Roosevelt's estate? Or that, once there, I'd receive a crash course in human rights and the urgent need for us all to accept and embrace our Universal Motherhood, which would change my whole outlook on life just as I was starting to think about this book?

See, you just never know what's around the corner. The *Poughkeepsie Journal* article inspired a woman named Barbara Henszey to e-mail my dear friend Kenny Zimmerman—one of my tribal elders and a fashion legend—for help getting in touch with me. Just days after the article appeared, Kenny forwarded me this e-mail:

From: Barbara Henszey
Date: July 13, 2010 8:55:22 PM EDT
To: Kenneth Zimmerman
Subject: Eleanor Roosevelt Center

Kenny,

The Eleanor Roosevelt Center in Hyde Park celebrates all the remarkable elements of ER's legacy, but its overall visibility is weak.

Kenny, I know you are a good friend of Kelly Cutrone. It struck me the other day that she and Eleanor Roosevelt might have been great friends. Kelly's book is full of poignant inspiration and activist wisdom, the hallmarks of ER's journey. Do you think Kelly might have an interest in contributing to the Center? I would appreciate any input—from brainstorming to assistance in planning an event. Perhaps when Kelly is at her weekend home, we could meet for an hour at Eleanor's Val-Kill home in Hyde Park.

If Kelly is not able to help at this time, I would love to give her and her daughter, Ava (and you and Arlene) a tour through the grounds. It's a most magical place.

Best,

Barbara

Reading this, I felt as though I'd been hit on the head with a coconut. I mean, Eleanor Roosevelt and Kelly Cutrone? *Whaaaaaaaaaat?!* I was simultaneously curious and elated that anyone would think Eleanor and I would have been friends, even though I knew almost nothing about her or what she accomplished in her life (but it certainly sounded fancy). I accepted the invitation partly because I was flattered, and partly because this woman Barbara seemed like she was stabbing around in the dark and needed some help. Maybe I could at least get her some free publicity for the estate.

Ava and I decided to visit Val-Kill the day before I was scheduled to fly to Toronto for a retreat with the Indian-born guru Sri Devi Amritanandamayi Ma, commonly called Amma, for whom I'd been consulting on media and branding. (To be honest, I don't really think Amma needs my help with anything, but she knows I love to work more than meditate, so she's been nice enough to throw me a bone.) This should have been my first clue that this would be no ordinary weekend in the country. The morning started off simply enough. When we awoke at my country house, my daughter and I walked down to the lake for a swim. It was one of those perfect Norman Rockwell scenes when you see the promise of life blooming in vibrant relief all around you.

I remember looking at Ava as she skipped up the path ahead of me after our swim, sun streaming through her hair. *There won't be many more summers when she's going to walk like a little girl,* I thought, *and when she's going to want to go for a swim with me.* Right before my eyes, there she was, growing up. I felt like an old sage in the forest, aware as I took in all her beauty and her youth that these days, and *my* days, were more than limited. My days as the mother of a young girl and then a teenager, and my days as a woman on this planet. I would be dead soon; there was no avoiding this thing called death. Don't get me wrong; I'm not planning on dying in five years or anything—and if I do, I guess I'll seem really psychic!—but as I gazed at my daughter through a prism of different perspectives, both short and long, I felt my awareness of everything heighten. If *cherish* and *psychically imprinted* had sex, they would be the parents of this feeling. Before I knew it, tears were streaming down my face.

This seems like a good time to set something straight. I know I called my first book *If You Have to Cry, Go Outside*, but what I meant was, it's not professional to let your emotions get the best of you in the workplace. I actually believe that if you're crying from gratitude, you can do it anywhere (though it's still better to not do it at the office). That day, watching Ava, I knew I was in a state of grace. I've never taken acid, but everything around me seemed tinged; I felt with every pore of my body the sheer amount of beauty, tenderness, and abundance in every breath and every interaction on this earth. The thing about states of grace is that they tend to announce themselves suddenly, with the backing of an angelic choir or maybe in a thunderbolt. It's usually pretty clear that something special's happening. Most of the time these moments are triggered by really simple things, as mine was, and maybe the moment itself is the entire teaching. The Divine could've just been reminding me to cherish having a child like Ava, for whom I'd manifested a country house as a single mother, so that she and I could have a more intimate relationship with nature.

I didn't know I was being prepared for a much larger teaching, one that would last for weeks. When Mira Alfassa, or The Mother—my longtime teacher and guru—was in her body, she sent certain students to other gurus to learn lessons they needed at certain times. Recently, I've felt that Amma is like one of The Mother's sisters who came to get me for the weekend—a very long weekend that has lasted over two years. The Mother and

her spiritual partner, Sri Aurobindo, were very focused on trans-
forming the self from the inside out—changing mind, life, and
body into channels of Divine consciousness—and Amma is also
focused on this, but in a more outwardly collaborative way. (I
believe she and The Mother are just differentiated aspects of the
same Divine being—that the Universal Mother has many faces.)
Amma's currently one of the greatest living examples of the
Divine feminine force in full effect. In addition to being a great
humanitarian, she has toured the planet for more than thirty-five
years hugging millions upon millions of people (over 30 million
to date). In fact, she sometimes spends up to twenty hours sitting in one place without so much as a meal or a bathroom break,
receiving anyone who wants to see her.

I would no sooner arrive on the grounds of Val-Kill than I'd realize I was in a sacred space. And by end of the weekend it would be
fair to say that Eleanor Roosevelt, Amma, The Mother, and Wonder
Woman—all great teachers—had had their way with me.

PART II: DEAR ELEANOR ROOSEVELT, I THINK I LOVE YOU

Val-Kill looks like a proper estate. It is breathtaking and majestic,
an American take on an impressionist painting. Of course, all of the
grace I'd felt walking to the lake that morning was soon shattered
when I showed up my normal fifteen minutes late and proceeded
to plow my SUV into several orange cones in the parking lot, infuriating two female-ish (and that's a compliment) park rangers.
Luckily, Barbara was there to receive Ava and me, because otherwise we probably would've been turned away. (I should really
give you a tip here about first impressions, but I'm not the one to

speak to those.) Before our tour, we were ushered into a screening room to watch a documentary about Eleanor's life.

This is when it all started to come together. As the film rolled, it hit me that Eleanor Roosevelt was a feminine force of superhigh consciousness and compassion, the counterpart to her husband's famous political consciousness and ambitions. Although most other First Ladies in history have sat behind their husbands, Eleanor and Franklin were really something (in addition to being cousins). In fact, to me they were a great example of Shiva Shakti, or the tantric balance of masculine and feminine dimensions collaborating to create tremendous life energy and transcendental awareness. I began to firmly believe that Amma and The Mother sent me to Val-Kill for a reason. They wanted me to meet their sister Eleanor.

One of my first symbiotic touch points with Eleanor was the opening scene of the documentary, when she stated that every powerful woman needs a home in the country to retreat to, a beautiful cottage where she can hear the sound of a brook. I knew this all too well, as I too have a beautiful cottage where I can hear the sound of a very cold spring. (Once you make some money, I highly recommend that you also buy or at least rent a country home where you can shower off the city each weekend; I think I'd be in jail by now if I didn't have one.) Actually, my home was just twelve miles from Eleanor's! And we had way more in common than that; like many powerful women in her time and ours, her sexuality was called into question. To be honest, I don't really know who she slept with, and I don't care. After learning more about her life, God bless her if she had time to sleep with anyone!

Eleanor Roosevelt was a woman ahead of her time. The First Lady is at least expected to live at the White House, which Eleanor couldn't be bothered with. She didn't give a fuck about sleeping with her husband; she had better things to do! It got to the point that it was actually *news* when she showed up. This was probably because, despite the fact that she bore President Roosevelt six children, her husband maintained a lover throughout their marriage—who also happened to be her best friend. But Eleanor was beyond all that. She and Franklin were actually a very modern couple by the time they hit the White House. I mean, they had a handful of kids, he was banging her best friend, and somehow they still found a way to work together for four terms! Even when they were no longer intimate, they remained close, with Eleanor functioning as Franklin's social conscience and generally keeping him in check. While he ran the country, she lived at Val-Kill, holding frequent press conferences on the issues of the day and writing a daily syndicated newspaper column called "My Day," which she used often to disagree with the president. She'd write the column every night at midnight from her room, no matter where she was.

In it, she revealed the consciousness of the true Universal Mother, full of clarity and compassion. Not only did she urge women to get out of the house and go to work; she fought for other groups too. The *New Yorker* penned a cartoon of the First Lady descending into coal mines to check on how the coal miners were doing. She'd call up her husband and say things like, "Franklin, it's unconscionable you're allowing lynching!" He'd say, "Why?" And she'd say, "Because, Franklin, it's not nice!" At one point he said to her, "Lady, this is a free country. Say what you think . . . Anyway, the whole world knows I can't control you."[1] To me, this sounds like an understatement, but a generous move by the president nonetheless.

I know no one's taking a vote, but to me Eleanor needs to be at the top of the list of First Ladies throughout history, and in fact of Americans as a whole. I want to hear her mentioned alongside George Washington and Ben Franklin. Seriously, she needs to be on our money!

After her husband died, Eleanor began her work with the United Nations, which is where one of her greatest accomplishments took place—she coauthored the Universal Declaration of Human Rights, which was signed by the General Assembly of the United Nations at the Palais de Chaillot in Paris in 1948. As the declaration's articles flashed on the screen that day, I knew I'd never read anything so fucking simple and beautiful and natural and true. It even said that requiring passports was a violation of our rights as humans—that we were all first and foremost citizens of the world. By this time, I knew Eleanor and I *definitely* would have been friends. Though I didn't know much about the document itself, I do believe I was born with an inherent understanding of human rights in my DNA. I mean, passports have always struck me as a huge "Fuck You"; why should I need a document to travel freely on this earth I was born on? I'm a citizen of the *world*, thank you very much.*

---

*Be honest. Haven't you ever felt this way before? Maybe you've even dated a European and been forced to stand in separate lines at customs? This happens to Ilario and me when we arrive at JFK with our daughter. I mean, *please.*

Dear President Obama,

I'm writing you this letter because I think it's absolutely deplorable that Eleanor Roosevelt is not on our money. In fact, why aren't there *any* women on our money? I mean, with the exception of Susan B. Anthony and Sacagawea—and nobody even uses silver dollars anyway. This seems like a mercy-fuck offering to the women's movement at best. I suggest we bump off one of those troublemaker presidents like Thomas Jefferson, who impregnated his slaves, and get Eleanor on instead. Alternatively, we could transfer Jefferson to the silver dollar and give Eleanor the nickel and the two-dollar bill, both of which he currently occupies. Or here's a better idea. Since every founding father came from a pioneering birthing mother, let's issue a feminine counterpart to *every* coin or bill, with pictures of people like Harriet Tubman, Rosa Parks, Betsy Ross, Margaret Sanger, Jane Addams, and Florence Nightingale. If women make over 70 percent of the buying choices in the average home, why aren't we on the money, even from a purely capitalistic standpoint? I mean, *Grover Cleveland* is on the thousand-dollar bill! Who the fuck is he?

Sincerely,

Kelly Cutrone

PS: While we're at it, I suggest we add two new people to Mount Rushmore: Eleanor Roosevelt and, with her, an indigenous person who made a difference in the history of our country, like Crazy Horse or Sitting Bull.

It all seemed so obvious. Of course we are all born into this world from a mother, and of course we all have a right to every particle on this planet. We should all be free and demand equal treatment under the law! Even gender and race are limiting.

I've always been in favor of the race of:
EVERYONE.
Would you like to join me?

(Let's get our birth certificates changed immediately. If and when you have a baby and they ask you to name its race, make sure you say, "Everyone.")

I was struck by how amazing it is that human beings still haven't mastered these *basic* concepts, despite the fact that the Divine has been sending people like Eleanor Roosevelt to us for millennia, from Krishna, Jesus, and Buddha to Gandhi, Rumi, Amma, and The Mother. Think about it. We have been on this earth for tens of thousands of years, and the Universal Declaration of Human Rights was just written 62 years ago! What is going on here? The progress of humanity is too fucking slow, and that is an understatement. As humans, we are inclined to repetition, not progression. It's easy to forget that 50 years ago, dark-skinned people still had to use separate bathrooms in some states in this country, and it was against the law for women to fly commercial planes.

I firmly believe that the United Nations needs a new PR team.

When the declaration was signed, the United Nations stated countries should "cause it to be disseminated, displayed, read and expounded principally in schools and other educational institutions, without distinction based on the political status of countries or territories." It was intended to blanket our civil institutions almost like the choking poster. But that never happened. Despite the fact that the Universal Declaration of Human Rights has been referred to as "the single most important reference point for discussions of how to order our future together on our increasingly conflict-ridden and interdependent planet,"[2] most of us have no idea it even exists, let alone have taken the time to read it as adults. And we are definitely not talking to our children about this.

The more I thought about it, the more I was embarrassed that I'd never really read the Universal Declaration of Human Rights, or learned much about Eleanor Roosevelt either. Here I was, an American woman from an iconic place (near the Yellow Brick Road, the birthplace of the suffragist/suffragette movement, and the Underground Railroad!) with little or no knowledge of many of the women who have fought with both fierceness and compassion for my rights, your rights, and others' rights throughout history. I hope I can inspire you to read about Eleanor and her work.

For posterity's sake, and the future's sake, on the next few pages we've included the Universal Declaration of Human Rights in its entirety.

THE UNIVERSAL DECLARATION OF HUMAN RIGHTS

Whereas recognition of the inherent dignity and of the equal and inalienable rights of all members of the human family is the foundation of freedom, justice and peace in the world,

Whereas disregard and contempt for human rights have resulted in barbarous acts which have outraged the conscience of mankind, and the advent of a world in which human beings shall enjoy freedom of speech and belief and freedom from fear and want has been proclaimed as the highest aspiration of the common people,

Whereas it is essential, if man is not to be compelled to have recourse, as a last resort, to rebellion against tyranny and oppression, that human rights should be protected by the rule of law,

Whereas it is essential to promote the development of friendly relations between nations,

Whereas the peoples of the United Nations have in the Charter reaffirmed their faith in fundamental human rights, in the dignity and worth of the human person and in the equal rights of men and women and have determined to promote social progress and better standards of life in larger freedom,

Whereas Member States have pledged themselves to achieve, in cooperation with the United Nations, the promotion of universal respect for and observance of human rights and fundamental freedoms,

Whereas a common understanding of these rights and freedoms is of the greatest importance for the full realization of this pledge,

Now, Therefore THE GENERAL ASSEMBLY proclaims THIS UNIVERSAL DECLARATION OF HUMAN RIGHTS as a common standard of achievement for all peoples and all nations, to the end that every individual and every organ of society, keeping this Declaration constantly in mind, shall strive by teaching and education to promote respect for these rights and freedoms and by progressive measures, national and international, to secure their universal and effective recognition and observance, both among the peoples of Member States themselves and among the peoples of territories under their jurisdiction.

Article 1. All human beings are born free and equal in dignity and rights. They are endowed with reason and conscience and should act towards one another in a spirit of brotherhood.

Article 2. Everyone is entitled to all the rights and freedoms set forth in this Declaration, without distinction of any kind, such as race, color, sex, language, religion, political or other opinion, national or social origin, property, birth or other status. Furthermore, no distinction shall be made on the basis of the political, jurisdictional or international status of the country or territory to which a person belongs, whether it be independent, trust, non-self-governing or under any other limitation of sovereignty.

Article 3. Everyone has the right to life, liberty and security of person.

Article 4. No one shall be held in slavery or servitude; slavery and the slave trade shall be prohibited in all their forms.

Article 5. No one shall be subjected to torture or to cruel, inhuman or degrading treatment or punishment.

Article 6. Everyone has the right to recognition everywhere as a person before the law.

Article 7. All are equal before the law and are entitled without any discrimination to equal protection of the law. All are entitled to equal protection against any discrimination in violation of this Declaration and against any incitement to such discrimination.

Article 8. Everyone has the right to an effective remedy by the competent national tribunals for acts violating the fundamental rights granted him by the constitution or by law.

Article 9. No one shall be subjected to arbitrary arrest, detention or exile.

Article 10. Everyone is entitled in full equality to a fair and public hearing by an independent and impartial tribunal, in the determination of his rights and obligations and of any criminal charge against him.

Article 11. (1) Everyone charged with a penal offense has the right to be presumed innocent until proved guilty according to law in a public trial at which he has had all the guarantees necessary for his defense. (2) No one shall be held guilty of any penal offense on account of any act or omission which did not constitute a penal offense, under national or international law, at the time when it was committed. Nor shall a heavier penalty be imposed than the one that was applicable at the time the penal offense was committed.

Article 12. No one shall be subjected to arbitrary interference with his privacy, family, home or correspondence, nor to attacks upon his honor and reputation. Everyone has the right to the protection of the law against such interference or attacks.

Article 13. (1) Everyone has the right to freedom of movement and residence within the borders of each state. (2) Everyone has the right to leave any country, including his own, and to return to his country.

Article 14. (1) Everyone has the right to seek and to enjoy in other countries asylum from persecution. (2) This right may not be invoked in the case of prosecutions genuinely arising from non-political crimes or from acts contrary to the purposes and principles of the United Nations.

Article 15. (1) Everyone has the right to a nationality. (2) No one shall be arbitrarily deprived of his nationality nor denied the right to change his nationality.

Article 16. (1) Men and women of full age, without any limitation due to race, nationality or religion, have the right to marry and to found a family. They are entitled to equal rights as to marriage, during marriage and at its dissolution. (2) Marriage shall be entered into only with the free and full consent of the intending spouses. (3) The family is the natural and fundamental group unit of society and is entitled to protection by society and the State.

Article 17. (1) Everyone has the right to own property alone as well as in association with others. (2) No one shall be arbitrarily deprived of his property.

Article 18. Everyone has the right to freedom of thought, conscience and religion; this right includes freedom to change his religion or belief, and freedom, either alone or in community with others and in public or private, to manifest his religion or belief in teaching, practice, worship and observance.

Article 19. Everyone has the right to freedom of opinion and expression; this right includes freedom to hold opinions without interference and to seek, receive and impart information and ideas through any media and regardless of frontiers.

Article 20. (1) Everyone has the right to freedom of peaceful assembly and association. (2) No one may be compelled to belong to an association.

Article 21. (1) Everyone has the right to take part in the government of his country, directly or through freely chosen representatives. (2) Everyone has the right of equal access to public service in his country. (3) The will of the people shall be the basis of the authority of government; this will shall be expressed in periodic and genuine elections which shall be by universal and equal suffrage and shall be held by secret vote or by equivalent free voting procedures.

Article 22. Everyone, as a member of society, has the right to social security and is entitled to realization, through national effort and international co-operation and in accordance with the organization and resources of each State, of the economic, social and cultural rights indispensable for his dignity and the free development of his personality.

Article 23. (1) Everyone has the right to work, to free choice of employment, to just and favorable conditions of work and to protection against unemployment. (2) Everyone, without any discrimination, has the right to equal pay for equal work. (3) Everyone who works has the right to just and favorable remuneration ensuring for himself and his family an existence worthy of human dignity, and supplemented, if necessary, by other means of social protection. (4) Everyone has the right to form and to join trade unions for the protection of his interests.

Article 24. Everyone has the right to rest and leisure, including reasonable limitation of working hours and periodic holidays with pay.

Article 25. (1) Everyone has the right to a standard of living adequate for the health and well-being of himself and of his family, including food, clothing, housing and medical care and necessary social services, and the right to security in the event of unemployment, sickness, disability, widowhood, old age or other lack of livelihood in circumstances beyond his control. (2) Motherhood and childhood are entitled to special care and assistance. All children, whether born in or out of wedlock, shall enjoy the same social protection.

Article 26. (1) Everyone has the right to education. Education shall be free, at least in the elementary and fundamental stages. Elementary education shall be compulsory. Technical and professional education shall be made generally available and higher education shall be equally accessible to all on the basis of merit.(2) Education shall be directed to the full development of the human personality and to the strengthening of respect for human rights and fundamental freedoms. It shall promote understanding, tolerance and friendship among all nations, racial or religious groups, and shall further the activities of the United Nations for the maintenance of peace. (3) Parents have a prior right to choose the kind of education that shall be given to their children.

Article 27. (1) Everyone has the right freely to participate in the cultural life of the community, to enjoy the arts and to share in scientific advancement and its benefits. (2) Everyone has the right to the protection of the moral and material interests resulting from any scientific, literary or artistic production of which he is the author.

Article 28. Everyone is entitled to a social and international order in which the rights and freedoms set forth in this Declaration can be fully realized.

Article 29. (1) Everyone has duties to the community in which alone the free and full development of his personality is possible. (2) In the exercise of his rights and freedoms, everyone shall be subject only to such limitations as are determined by law solely for the purpose of securing due recognition and respect for the rights and freedoms of others and of meeting the just requirements of morality, public order and the general welfare in a democratic society. (3) These rights and freedoms may in no case be exercised contrary to the purposes and principles of the United Nations.

Article 30. Nothing in this Declaration may be interpreted as implying for any State, group or person any right to engage in any activity or to perform any act aimed at the destruction of any of the rights and freedoms set forth herein.

In fact, I could fill this entire book with the names of great women who understood that, true to its title, normal gets you nowhere. For example, Margaret Sanger, who fought her whole life to bring women reproductive freedom via the birth-control pill, or Rosa Parks, who on a fateful December day in Montgomery, Alabama, in 1955 could *not* take being normal one more second and exploded like a phoenix, saying, to paraphrase: "Go fuck yourself. I'm not riding in the back of the bus anymore!" Or the former slave and antislavery activist Harriet Tubman, a fucking badass who not only saved herself from slavery, but, operating out of a house not far from where I grew up, helped about seventy other slaves escape, always armed with a revolver. Later in her life, when she had brain surgery to repair damage done by an injury from her slave days, she refused anesthesia and instead literally *bit a bullet* while they cut open her skull. If that's not a Divine being, I don't know what is!

These women are the real deal—incarnations and aspects of the Universal Mother who embody a true and ancient femininity that is ruthless and compassionate, fierce and loving, and the necessary counterpart to any masculine force, as well as being absolutely memorable—and we're not doing a good enough job teaching our daughters, and all of humanity for that matter, about these heroines. I want to hear people under forty talking about Eleanor Roosevelt. I mean, not in *one* recent speech, press conference, press release, nightclub, or news article have I seen or heard her name uttered! We need to pay these women the homage they deserve by continuing to fight the battles they started. Or at least we can make a shrine to them in our homes. In my new country house, I'm dedicating an entire wall to representations of the Universal Mother from every culture and belief system.

Because I believe a little of each of these extraordinary beings lives inside each of us, in our own souls—and the time has long since come for us to find and activate it.

In fact, I believe this force is *demanding* to be expressed in our time. I believe I was meant to take from Eleanor, and to pass onto you, a reminder of what it looks like when the feminine expresses itself in full on this earth, in all its compassion *and* tenacity. Luckily, the Divine Mother's not choosy; she'll pick anyone who will work for Her!* I could feel myself being initiated as a student of human rights for Her purposes. And let me tell you something, if you think your boss is bad, you should try working for *Her*—she is one relentless bitch, she will give you lashings, and by the way she has no HR department.

PART III: WELCOME TO UNIVERSAL MOTHERHOOD (ALMOST EVERYTHING COMES FROM A MOTHER)

It was Saturday evening, and my mind was already blown out. It had started with the Norman Rockwell acid trip with Ava and blossomed into a robust afternoon of human rights education; frankly, by dinnertime I was just happy to be back at my cottage watching TV.

I knew it wasn't a coincidence that I was scheduled to fly to Toronto the next day to join Amma and her swamis (who are like monks; they've set aside worldly pursuits to devote

---

*I believe the Divine particularly likes to infiltrate pop culture. And when it's interpreted properly in pop culture, whether in *Schindler's List*, *Wings of Desire*, *Devi*, or charitable anthems by Bob Geldof and Quincy Jones, it's unforgettable.

their lives full-time to the service of the Divine). In fact, I knew in every fiber of my being that these experiences would be directly connected. Before even boarding my plane to Toronto, I felt separated out from the world of human beings, like I was lying in the lap of the Divine Mother, helpless but to receive Her teachings. As if to confirm this, after landing in Toronto, I hit the town with a few friends, and everywhere we went, I saw fragments of Amma's name in street signs and advertisements. *AMMA*, the letters on a billboard would say, or *J'ama*, a café sign would read. It got to be so ridiculous that I started taking pictures.

By the time I returned to my hotel room later on, I felt on top of the world. Maybe this would be a proper and relaxing vacation after all. I was happy to be away from work, taking a much-needed break in the presence of one of the world's greatest living gurus. I proceeded to undress and get into bed, as I would on any night.

Suddenly, I was seized by a feeling that translated in my head into a clear female voice. I knew immediately that it was Her, the Divine Mother, and that She was speaking to me as Amma. She said she wanted to talk about the state of humanity.

You realize that this evolution has been going on for over ten thousand years, She said, offhand and casual, almost as if saying, "Hey, you got a second? Can we have a chat?" *People are going around in circles,* She continued. *They don't want to change. And I need your help.*

"There is nothing I can do to help you," I heard myself saying aloud, almost desperately. "I *cannot* help you. Look at me. I can barely help myself! I don't even understand why we're all still alive. Why don't you just flip this, like you did Atlantis?" (If you have time, look up Atlantis and Lemuria . . . fascinating.)

At this point in my life, even *I* knew no one truly wanted to be Divine. Look around. Human beings like to have one foot with God and the other with darkness; we like to spend our days saying, *I'm such a nice person, let me help you,* and our nights thinking, *Let's get fucked up. I want more money. Mmm, this tastes good!* Most people want Divine beings to do the spiritual work for them—that's why they give their religious institutions money, so their rabbis, priests, or swamis will pray *for* them. It's the same reason we elect politicians—so that *others* can set the laws and govern us and we can go about our business.

But again, I'm not asking you to do what everyone else is doing, or what's normal.

The voice spoke to me again. *Of course you can help,* it said.

And then things got worse.

During the next few hours, I would be made to physically experience the pain in the hearts of humanity, as if Amma were saying to me, *Do you want to feel it?* and then laying me down naked on a wooden bed, binding my arms, and cranking up the pain with a wheel—*crank, crank, crank!* It was like a primitive torture chamber of empathetic consciousness.

At one point, in a state of pure desperation, I called a friend in India, a sage I've turned to in many moments of spiritual tumult throughout my life. He didn't seem alarmed by my tears. "You're in a state of Divine feminine," he told me. "You're seeing the world through eyes of God—it's almost like you have

God's consciousness inside of you." (Obviously, I don't believe in this whole thing about humility and not talking about one's spiritual experiences. *Woo hoo, don't ever equate yourself with God!* Well, why *wouldn't* you want to equate yourself with God? The highest thing you could say about yourself is that you recognize there is a Divine source of energy living inside of you that wants to express itself.)

What I learned that night can be summed up like this. We have been programmed in this world to accept the suffering and devastation of other beings on an epic scale, not just around the world, but in our own fucking backyards. We are *all* suffering, and suffering deeply in our hearts. And our chaos, confusion, pain, and unfulfillment are manifesting outwardly in devastating ways. We know that Mother Nature can't hold us the way we're behaving with her, overusing and abusing her resources. We *know* the world is becoming a more violent place. Yet we continue in the dance of repetition—we refuse to evolve as a species. A long time ago, someone said to me, "Insanity is doing the same thing twice and expecting different results."

It just so happened that Eleanor knew this too. She was the First Lady in the time of the Great Depression, and she had more than one answer. She called on all young Americans to show compassion and leadership (yes, she even called on men to exercise their Universal Motherhood!). In her autobiography, she wrote:

The future will be determined by the young and there is no more essential task today, it seems to me, than to

bring before them once more, in all its brightness, in all
its splendor and beauty, the American Dream, lest we
let it fade, too concerned with ways of earning a living
or impressing our neighbors or getting ahead or finding
bigger and more potent ways of destroying the world
and all that is in it.[3]

By the American dream, I do not believe Eleanor meant three
SUVs and a McMansion. I believe she meant the fundamental
right of all beings to pursue their intuitive dreams and their best
selves, and an equanimity and compassion of spirit. Eleanor, like
Amma, had faith in the power of the smallest acts of individual
compassion to change the world and humanity. She was *not* apa-
thetic, even as the world seemed to burn all around her. Eleanor
also wrote:

I learned . . . while I was groping for more and more
effective ways of trying to cope with community and
national and world problems, that you can accomplish
a great deal more if you care deeply about what is
happening to other people than if you say in apathy or
discouragement, "Oh, well what can I do? What use is
one person? I might as well not bother."[4]

That night in my hotel room, Amma took Eleanor's teachings
even farther. She wanted me to know—to feel—that the world's
pain was not just starvation or homelessness, that we are *all* holding pain in our hearts. Like rats in a lab, many of us have just figured out, through cheap entertainments like the mall, meds, and

men, how to navigate around and ignore the deep dark corners in our minds and bodies.

After several hours of empathetic, excruciating exploration of the suffering of humanity compliments of Amma (literally), I collapsed on my back on the bed and fell into a deep sleep, prostrating myself in a state of humility, acceptance, and even gratitude for this wild, strange trip I'd been taken on. I knew I'd received a rare gift and a powerful teaching. I mean, I know I've said the truth hurts, but this was ridiculous!

I awoke the next morning in quite a state; in my delirium, I actually put on a red shirt—the first time I've worn color in years. I left my boutique hotel in downtown Toronto and caught a cab to the airport Sheraton, where Amma was hosting her retreat. I knew it was going to be a big day, just like it had been a big night. I had barely gotten through the front door when the voice came back.

Now, this is important, are you listening? I want you to feel MY response to the suffering, it said.

All of a sudden, in my hands, my shoulders, and every other part of my being, especially my heart and eyes, I was overwhelmed—drowned, consumed—by love and compassion. Standing inside this unremarkable Sheraton in Canada, all I could see was beauty all around me. If this had been a sci-fi movie, my eyes would've been shooting laser love beams that instantly disintegrated people's pain. It was such an intense feeling that my mortal body, which is *not* in a state of pure love and compassion, had a hard time physically accommodating it. I ran into a fellow devotee who had come to see Amma with his wife, and their love was palpable.

"You seem like you love each other so much," I said.

He nodded. "She's my goddess. I even bathe her feet in milk and ghee." (FYI, that's the way Amma's swamis bathe *her* feet.)

I thought to myself, *This is true Divine love.* For the second time in two days, I started crying hysterically, overwhelmed to see there were people still living like this in what often seemed like a hopeless world. As I made my way into the hall, I was vibrating with so much love and compassion that I physically ached.

I looked around furiously for somewhere to disappear and meditate or at least calm down and sit quietly in a corner, away from where Amma was holding court. I was forced to dive underneath a folding table where devotees were lining up to sign up to work at one of Amma's soup kitchens. Actually, the table was being manned by a friend of mine from northern California. She looked down at me with big, knowing eyes.

"It's okay. Hide under here," she whispered. "I know that feeling. Amma's done it to me too."

Once tucked away, I resumed my tears. I've learned that when these things happen, you can't try to figure them out. You just have to go along with them. Because once the mind gets involved in trying to process everything, it gets in the way. So there I sat, Amma's erstwhile branding specialist and a total blithering idiot, sobbing underneath a folding table at the Sheraton in Toronto in a complete state of love and compassion. At first I thought it was an altered state—but now I'm thinking maybe it was my true state, and I've just chosen to live the rest of the time in an altered reality. I'm not yet sure.

After a while, my swami—the one who had originally asked me two years ago to work with him and Amma—ducked under the table.

"What are you doing?" he asked.

"I'm just so filled with love and compassion," I replied.

"When was the last time you had a chai latte?" he inquired. "Get up. Let's take a chai."

We took a chai, and then he took me in to see Amma for darshan. In stark contrast to what she'd put me through the night before, she was—and is—this incredibly smiley, beatific being. Most people who come to see her ask for help with something specific—their ego, or buying a new house, or their health. But I put my head in her lap and screamed silently, *Make it stop!! End this teaching! I'm exhausted already!*

She picked me up, stared straight at me, and put her third eye to mine, almost laughing.

I knew then that I was no longer living in the world that had brought me here—that I'd been given a new one. Of course, this is what all the best, most profound teachings do. They kill you. I knew I'd never look at other human beings quite the same way again, nor would I return to my former ignorance. I was suddenly full of a new urgency to help myself and others become stronger, better, more profound. I knew I'd still battle the same slothlike human laziness that is totally resistant to change and growth—sometimes I just want to chill out, as you probably do too—but I'd also been shown, or made to *feel*, that there is so much work still to be done on this earth.

The Divine is demanding we become proactive to stop the suffering of humanity.

To do this, we don't have to go away for a spiritual weekend, book a ticket to an ashram, or even visit Val-Kill to learn about Eleanor Roosevelt. The tools you need are already inside of you, just waiting for you to call on them. Ruthlessness, fierceness, strength, love, compassion, and courage exist within *all* women—and all men too! We live in a society where our ancient powers of the feminine are still marginalized, where women are programmed to shut up and show up as arm candy for men, and where the lessons of beings like Eleanor Roosevelt have *not* caught on. (I guarantee that most women can name three famous supermodels, though.) We are being summoned to change over to a new way of being feminine. It's time for us to follow the example of women like Eleanor, The Mother, and Amma and unleash our Divine Motherhood into the world.

The feminine needs to represent itself accurately, integrally, and completely. Because the quicker we get into owning our innate powers of ruthlessness, fierceness, compassion, and sweetness, being truly honest and equal, speaking up for ourselves, and doing good for the world (*and* having great sex!), the faster the planet will heal, and the faster we'll all be able to get the hell out of here! We need to make "love" and "compassion" into active verbs, and we *all* need to embrace our Universal Motherhood—which, luckily, male or female, we can all do easily! As Amma has said, "The essence of motherhood is not inherent in women who have given birth. It is inherent in both men and women. It is an attitude of the mind."

And here we go.

I flew back to New York the next morning and went straight to the office, where I was unfortunately forced to fire an employee who was taking a shower in a back bathroom instead of sitting at her desk. Actually, I fired five people that day: It's still referred to as the "Bloodbath at People's Revolution." Later, I spoke on a panel with Little Steven from *The Sopranos* and the E Street Band at the New Music Seminar. After that, exhausted, I went to the Mercer Hotel for an omelette.

On the outside, it was business as usual. My life was demanding to go on on its own terms. But on the inside things were churning and burning. For the next few months, I'd find myself in tears in the most inappropriate places, from my agent's office at William Morris to meetings over a TV deal. I couldn't shake the power of my experiences at Val-Kill and in Toronto. My soul was busy concocting a recipe, one I'll share with you (since I know cookbooks are really hot right now):

How to Awaken Your Universal Motherhood = Consciousness + Compassion + Love in Action. (Oh, and don't forget to add a dash of ruthlessness.)

Here's a quick physics lesson. Matter—a word that comes from the Latin word *mater*, meaning "mother," by the way—is only matter because atoms agree to continually vibrate in harmony in order to form the chair you're sitting on and the ground on which your house stands. Well, I believe we're being called in this moment to harmonize *ourselves* too—to agree to continually vibrate with consistency, to repeat the same loving and compassionate actions every day in order to help ourselves and our species progress. It's not always easy, I know. When I'm short on compassion, I like to literally imagine myself as the mother of all beings—to behave as if everything, from a seal in the Arctic to a charming baby to a mass murderer, came through me. This is what it means to be a Universal Mother: to walk down the street beaming love and compassion, feeling no separation from anyone or anything else.

In other words, it doesn't mean you have to like everything you see. It just means you have to recognize you're not different from it.

FIVE

COMPASSION IS IN FASHION

No matter how rich we are, as long as we are not
prepared to be compassionate towards the poor, we
are truly living in utter poverty. Such people are the true
destitutes in the eyes of God.

—Amma

Over the years, I've received thousands of letters from young people who want to get into the fashion business; others ask me for clothing or interview advice or even how to handle a breakup. But not one has *ever* asked, "Can you tell me how I can help make a difference in my community?" I guess most people just don't see compassion as a chic thing to aspire to. They see it as something hippies do, or something the superrich do as a tax break, or something unemployed twenty-somethings do while trying to figure out their next move. Don't get me wrong. Fashion is worthwhile and powerful, and can turn Cinderellas into supermodels. But it's not attractive to have the spoils of this world and not feel for people who don't. I believe everyone who breathes the air of this earth, regardless of their job or their bank account, must give back more than just carbon dioxide.

I'm shocked now at how, with the exception of a few days or weeks of my life, my blinders have allowed me—a sensitive and aware person—to walk by my fellow humans in distress without noticing or helping them. I'm not alone. Most of us are taught by our parents to turn away from people in the street who are in desperate need of help! We're told to keep walking, to "mind our own business." We learn to pass by unspeakable things and situations without ever stopping, whether it's a mother hitting her child at a Wal-Mart or a homeless person starving or freezing on the street while we're on our way to American Apparel to get a two-for-one special on T-shirts. We're fed meat at every meal, but nobody would eat a ShopRite steak if they saw how the animals were treated! From a young age, we're programmed to believe that to be *normal* means not fighting the injustices all around us. Well, I don't believe we can kid ourselves anymore.

In order to have a full life, one's life must be *full*—of struggle, strife, glory, victory, living, education (both book and street), and, most important, one another. We need to connect and relate to all the others on the planet. We live in a world that's full of everything, yet we walk by homeless kids on the street! Do you see the disconnect? Not to sound 1960s, but isn't it time to "Stop, children, what's that sound, everybody look what's goin' down"? We shouldn't just accept destruction and individual devastation as normal everyday occurrences. Only when we start to attune to what's really happening all around us can we start to transform it. If you have the time to go out to a bar with your friends four times a week, you can go to a soup kitchen at least once. In fact, call me up, and I'll go with you.

I now believe that in order to have a balanced life, you have to do something *every week* for other people or your community— that making a difference should be on par with making love or making money. I'm not saying that just getting up in the morning, going to work, and doing your best can't be a service to your community; after all, people need jobs, and the fashion industry, for example, employs people from the shipping, trucking and freight industries to the garment district and definitely keeps the employees of Starbucks afloat. But it's no longer enough to just have a job. Doing good is not the exclusive responsibility of cute nonprofit vegan kids. We *all* have to have a HEART:

Health: If you're going to die young like Jimi or Janis, you're only temporarily helpful to the world. We have a genetic responsibility to live longer than the previous generation.

Earth: Protect and be connected to this earth. In other words, have your feet on the ground and your ears to the sound. I'm talking about recycling. Water. Power. Government. Safety. Violence. Neighborhoods.

Art: There is a calling and demand for beauty, even in the ugliest places. Art is a *need* of civilization. Bringing beauty into a place full of pain and suffering is compassionate and productive.

Revolution: Transform through action. Fight for truth like you fuck: with passion, commitment, blindness, and openheartedness.

Truth: Act when every one of your cells is saying *yes*. To me, there's no point in fighting unless you feel called. There are many injustices that I'm just not called to fight against. Who *do* I feel called to fight for? Young women and gay men. Everyone has different talents, but we're all called to fight for something. We're like a Divine football team: God made quarterbacks, linemen, safeties. So you better fucking take your position.

In our twenties, our time is mostly taken up with getting a job, finding an apartment, paying the rent, dealing with four roommates, finding someone to have sex with, partying, and then realizing, *Oh my God, I have to get up and go to work again*? In this period of your life, you may be very self-indulgent; I was. When I first moved to New York, I wasn't the most compassionate or well-informed person. I was consumed with having a wild time and thought mostly about myself. Thinking about Kelly was actually a pretty full-time job, between late nights out in clubs in the East Village and long mornings recovering, so I'd be ready to do it all over again. I got caught up in the video game we're all brainwashed into playing, consumed with chasing a nice apartment and a hot guy and a fancy wedding and more money and power. But none of that made me feel good, and it still doesn't. So eventually, I learned to use my time differently, and *better*.

Amma says that there are two kinds of poverty. One is caused by lack of love, and the other is caused by lack of money. She teaches that if we can cure the first, the second will not exist. To that end, she's directed her devotees to be mindful of homeless people in their own communities. Let's face it. Americans are always talking about disasters in other countries, but we have the highest rate of violence against women and children in the Western world and sixteen thousand homeless kids in New York City alone! Where are they? Why don't we see them? Are their moms selling them for crack? Are they being kept as massage slaves in some cramped storefront in Manhattan?

KELLY FROM THE BLOQUE

Last year, inspired by Amma and the example of Eleanor, I was moved to become more proactive in my own neighborhood. In fact, I even made up a new name for myself; Kelly from the Block (or *Bloque*). I'd often ordered extra meals at dinner to give away to the homeless on the walk home, but now I started making this a more regular thing. There is a man who lives in a stairwell around the corner from me. One night, walking back to my apartment with my daughter and her father, all of us incredibly well fed, I popped my head into the stairwell. "Hi, I'm your neighbor," I said. "I'm wondering, is there anything that you need?" The man was about sixty-eight years old and kind of out of it. He grabbed me and said, "Yeah baby! I need a kiss from you!"

Okay, so sometimes people aren't ready to accept your help at the exact moment you're ready to give it. In New York, people get used to being on their own and not accepting help, since in this big, rich city, there often seems to be so little compassion available. I told the man I couldn't kiss him, but that I'd be happy to help him find a shelter or get him some food. He said no—that he was okay. (Three months later I told this story to Amma herself; she laughed hysterically. I think she sees the beauty and humor in everything.)

I didn't stop trying, though. Everyone sleeping on the streets of New York is someone's child, and once I started to reject the idea that I'm just supposed to mind my own business while people suffer, I became unable to walk by anyone in need without stopping. This can be tricky in downtown Manhattan, because the "haves" and the "have-nots" tend to sport similar looks (I guess deconstruction and devastation sometimes go hand in hand).

One day, leaving the SoHo Grand Hotel with my trainer, I locked eyes with a man who was either a cool artist or a homeless person. What I noticed first was that his eyes were on fire. I watched as he glanced over toward the garbage cans—he was possibly hungry, but also discreet and elegant. Then I saw him pause in front of a gallery window to look at some art. I realized he was reading the reviews in the window, as if determined to stay connected to this earth and its culture. I bolted toward him. My trainer, who was just thrilled to see me in a full-on cardio sprint, followed close behind. When we caught up to the man, he turned around, and I saw that he was not only beautiful, but powerful. He didn't look homeless; he looked like Adrian Brody's uncle!

It was obvious he hadn't yet crossed over into the realm of "here, but not there"—the place so many of society's forgotten retreat to, behind a wall that protects them from our callousness. This man was still on the bridge, where a work rehabilitation program or even just a fucking hug could have been the thing that saved his life. I asked if he wanted my help. I even told him I knew he was someone's child and that I recognized the Divine in him. It was weird, but as I said this, I started crying, overwhelmed by the urge to grab his hand and walk him to a safe space, to pull him back to my side of the bridge, back from somewhere over there and into the now.

He glanced at my trainer and told him in Spanish to tell me that he was fine, that everything was okay. I decided to at least offer him some money, but then realized, fuck, I *had* no money! So I borrowed a $20 from my trainer, who was blown away. (Granted, he'd only ever seen me cry doing squats at the gym.)

"This is something I'll remember for the rest of my life," he said, as we walked back to the hotel.

Even after this, I wasn't discouraged. Sure, I'd been hit on by one homeless guy and rejected by another, but I told myself I wouldn't stop keeping my eyes open and trying to fulfill my mission. If you're going to be a helpful being, you have to feel people's energy and act on your intuition—and you have to be ready to look like an idiot sometimes.

The next time I saw a homeless person, he was sitting on Grand Street with a sign that said "Homeless and hungry. Please help."

I stopped. "It's cold out. Can I get you something hot to drink?" I asked.

"Yes, I'd like a hot chocolate," he replied.

"C'mon," I gestured toward a deli. "Let's go get one."

"That's okay, baby," he said casually. "I'll just wait here."

As I walked away, he called after me to request a granola bar too. As I walked out of the deli with the homeless man's hot chocolate and granola bar, I ran into a friend of mine.

"What are you up to?" he asked.

"Oh, I'm just working for *that* guy!" I said.

Outside, the man with the sign accepted my offering with the air of a husband zoned out in front of the Super Bowl. He barely muttered, "Thanks."

I guess you can't necessarily expect a lot of gratitude when you wait on homeless people. If you want positive reinforcement, thank-yous, and a marching band to publicize your generosity, this is not the right kind of charitable work for you to be involved in. Homeless people haven't read the latest Emily Post book and don't necessarily have the best manners. Which is actually a good reminder that we shouldn't just do these things to stroke our ego—we should do them because we *can*.

DO NOT ASK WHAT A PUBLICITY STUNT CAN DO FOR YOU; ASK WHAT YOU CAN DO WITH A PUBLICITY STUNT

Sometimes, when you start looking around and actually notice all the people and worthy causes that need your help, it can be overwhelming. You might feel like you can't possibly help them all, so why bother trying? What I have always done is to rely on my intuition. Where and when do I feel called to act? Sometimes you see someone suffering and you have a heartfelt moment of empathy, and other times God hits you on the back of the head and says, "You can't sit by and let this happen. You have to get up and do something or say something." Once you're in tune with that feeling, you can go toward it.

This is what people did in the 1960s, when the youth took to the streets and to college campuses to protest for equal rights or to end the Vietnam War. Fuck, in the '80s, they even rioted in Tompkins Square Park to protest the opening of the Gap! Nowadays, it saddens me to see that young people are more into drugs and money and fame; these things have completely hijacked youth culture. Instead of a thousand kids lined up to try out for the next *Bachelorette*, I'd love to see a thousand girls in bikinis lining up along the banks of the Hudson River on the West Side of Manhattan, looking really hot and holding signs that say, "We want to go for a swim! It's preposterous that we live on an island, surrounded by water, and we can't swim! It's hot, and so are we!"

I believe young people are the ones who can and must put an end to this. I want to see the youth rising up to say, "*No*, it is *not* okay that we can't swim in our water, and why aren't we studying the effects of all this pollution on our children? And while we're at it, it's *not* okay that we've put Indians on reservations! It's *not* okay that a plane flew through the fucking Pentagon and no one even knew it was coming!" Let's be honest: If a plane flew through the tent at one of my fashion shows, the designer would fire me immediately, even if it wasn't my fault. I know I've said the world will change when we change ourselves; that's why I named my company People's Revolution. But sometimes, our *selves* need a little kick-start.

When we start awakening to the suffering all around us, it can be hard to *not* speak out. Recently, I was in a business meeting with a Spanish client, the head of one of Europe's largest and most colorful brands, and we were talking about "celebrity gifting," which means giving free clothes to famous people so they'll appear in the weekly magazines wearing them. I have done this hundreds of times in my career. But suddenly it just sounded stupid and incredibly wasteful.

"You know what?" I said. "Celebrities have enough clothes. Why don't we gift fifty or seventy-five pieces to celebs and fashion editors and give the rest to the homeless?" I pointed out that winter was coming, and that the homeless would actually need clothes for warmth, not just to be on-trend for the season. Besides, we had literally hundreds and hundreds of extra pieces of clothing, everything from coats to sweatshirts to dresses. I didn't think this was such a crazy idea.

But you would have thought I'd suggested that aliens were waiting for us on the corner of 5th and 57th and we should fly off to open a new branch of their store in outer space. My client was totally offended and shocked. He looked me right in the eye and said, *"But that means there would be homeless people wearing our clothing!?!?!"*

"Well, yes, that's exactly what it means! But it also means your brand would be the brand with the vision, compassion, and confidence to dress the thousands of homeless teenagers in New York City who do not even have the luxury of shopping at a Salvation Army. In my opinion, that'd be the coolest campaign a clothing company could ever roll out."

Unfortunately, my client didn't see it that way. *Lamentablemente, mi cliente no verlo así.*

Another missed opportunity I've seen recently in the fashion industry is Fashion's Night Out, an annual evening of shopping launched by *Vogue* that was supposed to help reinvigorate the sagging retail industry in New York. Years ago, I might have had the time of my life at an event like this, but last year, in September 2010, it just didn't feel very festive to me. I spent the night running all over town with clients, and although most of the stores were mobbed, they didn't seem as if they were actually making money. Instead, it looked like thousands of women went out and got a blow dry, hired taxis, and got drunk. The taxi drivers made a lot of money, and the hairstylists made a lot of money, and the bars made a lot of money. I couldn't help but think that someone should have opened their store and said, "You know, last year was a horrible year for us. But tonight, we're going to feed homeless people in our store. Because we believe that compassion is in fashion."

Fashion is usually a very giving and charitable industry; designers and brands raise hundreds of thousands, even millions of dollars every year for charities like Dress for Success, the American Foundation for AIDS Research (AMFAR), and the Design Industries Foundation Fighting AIDS (DIFFA). But I believe that we, like every industry, can do more. Can you imagine if all of New York's fashion brands or banks banded together for one night, one week, or even two and put forth the same amount effort that they usually put into producing fashion shows or annual reports for their boards? They would most definitely change the entire city.

What we can do on our own is important, but what we can achieve by working together is even greater and absolutely necessary. For example, I'd like to see all companies stop work for twenty-four hours at least once a year to clean up their blocks, whether that means feeding people who are hungry or fixing the roads. What if every business located between Grand and Canal Streets and 6th Avenue and Broadway got together to arrange a series of meetings on how best to help the neighborhood, and then, beginning on Friday at around five and ending Monday at noon (since New Yorkers like to make money during the week) joined together and said, "We're going to change our block now." This would not be hard. With the kind of talent, labor, and money we'd have at our disposal, it would actually be very simple to transform a neighborhood in a weekend. Why aren't we all doing this? Maybe it's because most of us don't believe that our voice actually matters.

MAMA WOLF MEETS WILD TIGER

One of the best things about showing compassion to others is that the smallest acts of kindness come back to you. I literally owe the roof over my head to this mantra. Years ago, I was working on a project with a very high-end clothing designer. The brand's New York store was licensed, meaning it was owned by a third party and not the brand itself. This is how some brands can afford to expand quickly, especially in foreign markets. (It's not unlike Dunkin Donuts. You put up the sign, you agree to follow the creative direction of the brand, you purchase a certain amount of their products each year, and then you split the profits.) Anyway, this brand was trying to convince a very wealthy Asian woman named Kiko to license a store in Korea. Licenses are especially popular in Asia, since European and American companies don't necessarily understand the culture or have the staffing resources and the sizing is different.

I happened to know my client's New York store was not profitable and that as part of the deal the brand was going to try to convince this poor woman to throw money at it. This during a time when the designer was behaving erratically if not downright ridiculously, adding different brand extensions at a frenetic pace ("Today I'm making a whole golf collection! Tomorrow, ski coats!"). I soon became convinced my client was going to roll Kiko for about $30 million.

At the time, I'd never met Kiko and had no responsibility to look out for her. Actually, it was the opposite. I had a responsibility to my client to be discreet with all the information I knew about their brand. If I said everything that I really felt on a daily basis about how my clients run their businesses, I would have no clients. But for some reason, this potential deal really bothered me, and I couldn't stop thinking about it. I waited a few days before calling my mom for advice. "If you have that knowledge, you have to say something," she said matter-of-factly. I knew nothing about Kiko except that her family owned a lot of real estate in New York and she wore Junya Watanabe (you gotta love some Watanabe). But I took my mother's advice and called her, since by then I already knew not to put anything important in an e-mail.

Kiko came to People's Revolution, and we went to the back two rooms, which were my makeshift apartment. She was super-cool, beautiful, and privileged. I told her, without mincing words, that she was definitely about to lose a lot of money.

"You know," she said, nodding gravely, "everyone calls me the 'Wild Tiger' for a reason." (Here she made a menacing ges-ture.) She agreed she should pull out of the deal immediately. I had no choice but to also resign, since I'd betrayed my client's trust.

After that, Kiko and I became friends. One day when she stopped by my office, there was a considerable amount of noise upstairs; my neighbors were moving out.

"You *have* to have that apartment," Kiko said.

Unfortunately, I happened to know it cost $6,000 a month. But before I could protest, she pulled out her checkbook and wrote me a check for $40,000. I told her I'd never be able to pay her back; nor would I be able to afford the place when her money ran out.

"You're a smart girl. You'll figure it out," she said, unconcerned.

And she was right—I did. Eventually, I took over the second and fifth floors of the building as well.

I believe that all of the things you do for other people, you're actually doing for yourself. Life is like a bank account. Random acts of kindness, telling the truth, being loving, showing up for yourself and others—these are all deposits. Getting fucked up, fucking other people over, letting your ego lead your choices—the things we think are fun after eleven at night but don't seem so entertaining at eleven in the morning—are withdrawals. If we give more than we take, we progress. If we take more than we give, we regress.

This is why, since I opened People's Revolution in 1996, I've always chosen to represent two or three clients for free. In doing so, I'm showing the universe that I'm grateful for what I've been given—I'm making deposits into my bank account. After all, if I believe my talents are God-given, I have a responsibility to give them back to God. I hope you agree with this, whether you're a painter, a lawyer, a homemaker, or a maid. Whatever you do to contribute to this world, make money, and build a life for yourself, why not volunteer services to help others in your community too?

There's a saying, "There but for the grace of God go I." To me, this means that everything could flip, any day of the week. The thing that most repulses or scares us could be in our future, so we shouldn't be so quick to judge and ignore. We never know what the universe is going to deal us. Though it seems totally impossible, *you* could be that person you're walking by on the street or, more likely, the person who loses her job and needs a loan from a friend, a little compassion, or maybe a place to stay for a few weeks.

I've been the village girl from Syracuse, the penniless yogi with a shaved head out in L.A., and the black-haired fierce bitch taking over the runways, I dare say. It's important that no matter what your position, you savor and make the best of it—that you take from each reality what it has to offer you (and they all have something, trust me). And that you show compassion. After all, I refuse to be killed by your narcissistic psychic footprint.

SIX

I FOUGHT THE LAW AND THE LAW WON

There are three sides to every story: your side, my side, and the side of the truth.

—Ola Tungi, from the Peter Tosh documentary *Stepping Razor: Red X*

Did you know that in America you can actually make a career out of suing people? All you have to do is become the town crier, running around accusing people of things! Start by confronting someone and saying, "You stole $50,000 from me." The person will say, "No, I didn't." Then you say, "Yes you did." Then you call the police and file a report. "I did not steal from her. She's crazy!" the other person will tell the police. But too bad for them! The police *have* to let you file the report, and after that the other person will have to convince a jury of your peers that she did not steal $50,000 from you.

I don't know about *your* peers, but mine are fucking nuts. They're also in a bad mood, because they're probably losing money while they sit down at the courthouse on the jury hearing about your supposed $50,000. Do you think they give a shit? They're more interested in their BlackBerrys. This is why being litigious is easy money. As you move up the ladder in your career—and especially if you decide to start your own business—

you'll learn that you really need friends who are lawyers, because they speak a language called *law*.

For the record, the *law* has nothing to do with the *truth*.

Yet it is still the place we've decided to work out our grievances with each other. And to me, war is war, whether you've got a gun or a gavel in your hand. Still, it took me well over ten years of business to learn what I feel is one of the most important life lessons for you to hear and heed: Get. A. Lawyer.

As you might have guessed, I recently had a crash course in the law that shattered all remaining shards of my innocence with a hammer. This is why I now believe that when you go to work for someone, you should know what the labor laws are in your city before you draw your first paycheck. It's the wild, wild West out there, and I want you to be prepared.

SHE PUT THE CUNT IN CUNT-TRACT

Years ago, I represented a woman who shall remain nameless, but let's just say she is a horrible designer (while I make it a rule to only represent people I believe in, I'd hired an employee who brought along some of her own clients, the PR equivalent of bedbugs). When we stopped working together, she left an unpaid retainer of $35,000. There was no point in suing this woman for the $35,000 she owed me, because by this time I already knew how the system worked. If I dragged her to court, I'd owe $75,000 in lawyers' fees. So I held on to her ugly collection instead, hoping this might convince her to pay her bill. When she called me up wanting it back, I said, "Go fuck yourself. *Pay me* bitch."

She called the police. Unfortunately, we didn't have a clause in our People's Revolution contracts back then giving us the right to keep designers' samples until they paid their bill (now we do). So the police came to my office and confiscated the property; in their view, the unpaid $35,000 was a separate issue that had to be resolved in court.

I thought this was the end of the episode, and I was prepared to write off the money as a cost of doing business, literally so I'd never have to see this woman's terrifying face again. Little did I know she was only getting started. One day, I was sitting at my desk at the office when I heard a knock at the door. In walked a uniformed official bearing a yellow legal notice.

"Kelly Cutrone?" he asked. "You have been served."

If you haven't had the pleasure, let me explain: Being *served* means the state dispatches someone to physically hand you legal papers and confirm you have them in your possession—this typically happens in a divorce. But I wasn't being served divorce papers. My former client was suing me for stealing a portion of her collection which she valued at *one million dollars*. At first, I couldn't believe it. I mean, this was preposterous! Who did this bitch think that she was?

I went to court to give a deposition. A deposition is when the town crier's lawyers ask you whatever the fuck they want to. In fact, their job is to help you have a breakdown, so you look like a crazy person and their client (the *real* crazy person) looks good.

"Have you ever lied?" they might ask.

"Have you ever fired staff in front of other staff?

"Have you ever lost anything belonging to your clients?"

"Can you say with absolute certainty in your business that you have always painstakingly known where *everything* was?"

Lawyers don't care about the truth; they just want to *win*, and bill as many hours as possible. As the months went by, I was forced to appear in court again and again to file motions, and my own legal bills started to pile up: $10,000, then $20,000, then $40,000, then $60,000. On top of this, I was bringing in less money, because I was wasting my time in court instead of pitching new clients. At one point, my lawyer suggested I cut my losses and settle for $200,000. By this point I knew I was the losing person at the gambling table, but I would have sooner gone down on a burning ship than pay this woman shit. This was about *principle*. I was not about to give up.

On July 5, 2010, four years after being served, I was working with Amma in New York when I had to excuse myself to appear at a mandatory prehearing for the case, which was still dragging on.

"Where are you?" one of Amma's swamis texted me.

"In court," I typed. "A client is accusing me of stealing $1 million worth of her collection."

"Oh, good luck," he wrote back.

Good luck? I thought. *That's all he has to say?* Apparently, even swamis know the law has nothing to do with the truth.

My lawyer was terribly afraid I was going to act like a crackpot in court. In fact, he'd even asked a mutual friend of ours how she was possibly friends with me, since I was by now calling him routinely to shriek obscenities like, *"Go fuck yourself! We are not settling! I did not steal anyone's property! I have had everything taken from me in this industry! It will not take my principles and my liberties too!"*

He'd asked me *please, please* not to say anything inappropriate in front of the judge and to make sure I dressed appropriately too.

So I showed up in Donna Karan, with my hair pulled back. I was calm, since I'd been busy meditating all weekend with Amma's swamis. But the sight of my former client in the hallway, full of lies, put me over the edge.

"Every cent you steal from me is going to rot you," I hissed, boring my eyes right into her. "It is going to *hurt* and *rot* you."

She looked visibly nervous. At the last hearing, her lawyer had asked mine whether I was involved in witchcraft, since I was making his client physically ill. He demanded I refrain from staring at her.

"If she's going to accuse me of stealing $1 million from her, you'd better believe I'm going to stare at her the whole fucking time we're sitting here," I told my lawyer.

After all, when victims' families go to court to confront a perpetrator, they stare at the offender the whole time. How was this any different? This woman was trying to murder my business!

I proceeded into the judge's chambers with my lawyer—the parties go in one at a time to have their side heard—who was trying to calm me down. "She's a nice judge," he whispered, "and she likes fashion!" I thought she looked like Ann-Margret.

"Hello, Ms. Cutrone," she said.

"Hello, Your Honor," I replied.

"So what is going on here?" she asked.

I explained that I was a single mom who works very hard for her money, that I've worked for sixteen years for top names in the business—from Bulgari to Christie's Auction House to Vivienne

Westwood to Paco Rabanne—and that none of these people had ever accused me of stealing. I'd been fighting my former client for four years at a high cost to myself and my business, on *principle*. In fact, I'd already spent the equivalent of two years' worth of my daughter's private schooling.

The judge nodded. "I understand," she said. "But the problem is, if you go to court, you leave your fate to the jury. They might see a single mom, or they might see a powerful, tough-as-nails businesswoman. It just depends who you get."

I couldn't believe that even the *judge* was encouraging me to settle. She was in on it too! It was actually her job to discourage people from going to court, as court eats up the taxpayers' money! I stared up at the wall, where I saw the words "In God We Trust," and then looked down at the dollar bills visible through my clear clutch. That's when I had an epiphany that caused me to bawl my eyes out.

"Why does it say 'In God We Trust' on our money and on your wall?" I demanded. "Nothing here has anything to do with God *or* the truth!"

I used to think Justice was blindfolded so her other senses would be heightened—I mean, that's how it works in S&M; if you cover your eyes, you can feel and hear more. I also thought she was blindfolded because she wouldn't want to judge by appearances. Now I realize that is poppycock.

Lady Justice is blindfolded because she does not *want* to see the legal system. If she saw it, she would see it has nothing to do with the truth, and this would destroy her.

"I need some time to think about this," I said.

The truth was, I was beyond devastated. When I started out in business, I was an idealist with a capital "I." My business model was It's a Small World, i.e. the Disneyland ride. I thought everyone could just work together and make beautiful things and that none of my employees would ever quit and everything would be amazing. But that's not how the world is. Laws are arbitrary, after all. They were written because humans have agreed that they do not want to master themselves. So they appointed leaders to get together and do their dirty work for them. I mean, for most of the twentieth century it was illegal to give a blow job in New York state! Certain laws are for the best, of course, but the fact that someone can just waltz up to me and threaten my livelihood by accusing me of breaking the "law" seemed so ridiculous.

By the time we stood in the judge's chambers together, the two of us with our lawyers, I'd dispensed with all niceties.

"I will *only* offer you one number," I said. "And if you do not accept, I'll take this all the way to the end."

She wanted $100,000, but I told my lawyer to tell her to go fuck herself. The judge told her she'd have to come down, since she was lucky I was offering her anything.

"$58,000," I said. "*And that is it.* I would like permission to leave now, Your Honor, so I can get back to meditating."

I paid her the money over six months, since I didn't have enough to cover it in a lump sum. It's money that would have gone to my daughter's college education, and now it was going to this stupid lying bitch. All because *anyone* can accuse you of *anything*, and the burden is on *you* to prove you didn't do it.

I NOW BELIEVE THAT WHEN YOU DO BUSINESS WITH PEOPLE, YOU HAVE TO RECOGNIZE THEY ARE POTENTIALLY DANGEROUS TO YOU

Doing business with people is no different than moving to a big city. You can't just see every man as a potential boyfriend; you also have to see him as someone who could be dangerous to you at night. And if you open your own company, you should be aware that all those who pass through your doors, whether visitors, clients, messengers, or employees, are not just a potential boon to your business—they're also a potential menace. As you follow your intuition and pursue your dreams, you must be very careful about who you do business with. I mean, God forbid someone you've invited to your office slips on the ice, or a ceiling fan falls on their head, or you say something un-PC, or the elevator gets stuck and causes someone emotional trauma—being an entrepreneur is a scary business! Every time I raise my voice, I'm risking a labor case from a wounded underling.

In fact, several years ago, I was sued for stealing dog food from an employee! This was my favorite legal battle of all time. A senior employee had had a full-blown anxiety attack in the corner just four days before fashion week and required hospitalization. Needless to say, this totally screwed us over. I was producing twelve to fourteen shows and running showroom appointments—where buyers come to see the collection after the runway show and purchase it for their stores—for over a dozen designers. I ended up having to place two of my clients in other showrooms, since we were now short-staffed and there was no time to hire more help.* Somehow we survived, albeit with fewer clients, and six months later my anxiety-ridden former employee stopped by my office to pick up his bike and his dog food.

"Your bike? Your dog food?" I responded. "Well, the dog food we threw out. You left it here, and we were infested with mice. As for your bike, I have no idea where it is."

Well, he took me to small claims court. I went with my lawyer friend, Herman. "You have been accused of stealing fifty pounds of dog food," said the judge, clearly amused when I approached the bench with my former employee *and his mother,* whom he'd brought along for emotional support. (If you want to be entertained, you should spend the day in small claims court seeing the ridiculous things humans cannot resolve between themselves.)

"My former employee left rather abruptly with a medical condition," I told the judge, "and when he left, he left the dog food. I threw it out because it was attracting mice. And he never even asked my permission to bring his dog in the first place."

"And the bike?"

"Your Honor, look at me," I said. "Do I look like I ride a bike?"

The judge dismissed the case. But as long as I was there, I decided to see what was in it for me.

"Your Honor, I had *mice* in my McQueen shoes," I said. "Can I at least get some money out of him for the exterminator?"

---

* I'd just helped Marcus Wainwright and David Neville of Rag & Bone launch their brand, and now I had to ask them to seek other representation; they ended up with Denise Williamson and became the darlings of the industry.

SEVEN

THE NO MATTER WHAT CLUB

A true friend never gets in your way
unless you happen to be going down.
—Arnold H. Glasow

In today's disposable culture, we throw away people like we do razors, always assuming there's someone better out there to hang out with, or to work for—people who will never embarrass us, let us down or offend us. I see it all the time in my own life and others' lives, and even in my office. When one of my employees or one of her friends says something insensitive late at night after a few too many drinks, she spends the day on the phone putting out fires, judging or overreacting. I'll hear things like "Do you have any idea what you did last night?" or "Listen, I need my space, this isn't working for me," or "You betrayed me!" Just like we've been programmed to walk by homeless people lying on the street in desperation, we've been programmed to dump and discard friends anytime we're hurt or something inappropriate has been done to us. I hate to break it to you, babe, but *you*, too, will do things that horrify you and your loved ones in this lifetime! At certain times down the road, you probably won't even recognize yourself. Join the club. It's called *the human race.*

The truth is, is if we keep running away from everyone who hurts or betrays us, we will ultimately end up alone.

The evidence is mounting that we're suffering a crisis of friendship in our time. A 2006 study found that Americans' average number of confidantes dropped one-third between 1984 and 2004 (from three to two). Twenty-five percent of people said they had *no one* to talk to about important things! They also said they were relying more on their families for support. There's just one problem. As a professor of sociology named Rebecca G. Adams told the *New York Times* in 2009: "Friendship has a bigger impact on our psychological well-being than family relationships." And it's not just our psychological well-being; lack of friends has been linked to higher rates of viral disease, cancer, and even death! See, it *does* pay to be popular!

The famous Roman orator Cicero is one of my favorite philosophers on the subject of friendship:

> What can be more delightful than to have someone to whom you can say everything with the same absolute confidence as to yourself? Is not prosperity robbed of half its value if you have no one to share your joy? On the other hand, misfortunes would be hard to bear if there were not someone to feel them even more acutely than yourself. . . . Such friendship enhances prosperity, and relieves adversity of its burden by halving and sharing it. And great and numerous as are the blessings of friendship, this certainly is the sovereign one, that it gives us bright hopes for the future and forbids

weakness and despair. In the face of a true friend a man
[okay, a woman too!] sees as it were a second self. So
that where his friend is he is; if his friend be rich, he is
not poor; though he be weak, his friend's strength is his;
and in his friend's life he enjoys a second life after his
own is finished.[5]

Is it me, or has friendship lost some of the intensity it seemed
to enjoy two thousand years ago? You might be wondering: what
the fuck is a No Matter What Club? Well, it's something I've created for us out of a need for true friendship and intimacy.

**The No Matter What Club is a group of people who are
progressive, open, fearless, and courageous enough to agree
to truly be there for one another, *no matter what*.**

Think of it as a list of names you've tattooed on your mind
and heart. Possibly a few things could get someone kicked off
this list, like pedophilia or cannibalism. But for the most part,
these are the people you're choosing to take life's journey with,
through thick and thin, shame and excess, failure and victory.
It's kind of like what a marriage is supposed to be—except better, and purer.

In America, we tend to think of friends as social companions,
people to go to the movies with once or twice a month. But your
No Matter What Club is not just a list of people you work, meditate, go shopping, or even have sex with. These are people whose
team you're genuinely signing up to be on.

If you're anything like me, you've probably connected with
tons of people in friendship over the years. Maybe you've even

been lucky enough to love a few of these people (and I hope for your sake they've loved you back). It's possible you've told them you'd do anything for them. But think about it now. *Would* you? It's weird, because at the same time that our world is disposable, it's also strangely accelerated. So many of these people we throw away are the very same people we told, when we met them just four weeks earlier, that they were our new *best friend* and that we would *love them forever*! (American society's definition of "forever" is usually between four weeks and four years, whether we're talking about friendships, marriages, or jobs.)

Often I hear things like, "Oh, I know so-and-so. She's a great friend of mine." Oh really? But you've only known her three weeks! *Are* you really friends? *Do* you really love her? Why don't you try hanging out for at least a few months before you decide, because by then it's highly likely she's going to do something to freak you out or upset you. *Social acquaintance* is not the same as *friend*; we need to use phrases like, "I love you," "You're amazing," "I'll do anything for you," and "You're my new best friend," appropriately. We shouldn't just throw them out at the hostess stand when we're trying to get a good table.

Most of us are too quick to call people friends, too quick to say "I love you," and too quick to write people off forever. Instead, we need to accept that whoever we decide to truly love and call a friend will inevitably let us down in our lifetime. This is why we should be very exacting in our selection of who we will place in our No Matter What Club. The people you love most *will* hurt or destroy you on some level, whether it's in the immediate future or years down the road. So will your mother (if she hasn't already), your fiancé, your husband, and your child. It doesn't make them horrible, worthless, or unredeemable. It just makes them human beings.

Besides, I can promise you you'll do it right back to them. Especially when you're young and trying to figure out how to manifest and embrace your own power, a lot of mistakes are going to be made. There are so many distractions in the world that can take you down: vanity, greed, lust, envy, and yes, drugs and alcohol . . . you get it. Sometimes when we're in the middle of fucking these things, it makes it hard to be good friends. Drugs and alcohol, especially, turn us into marionette puppets; they pull our strings and make us do stupid, regrettable things. I don't know anyone who drinks, myself included, who hasn't at some point had to call a friend, play fill-in-the-blanks, and offer apologies for the night before.

When we see people in pain, whether it's from depression, heartbreak, or drugs and alcohol, we tend to back off, reverting to responses like, "I can't deal with her," or "She is so awful when she drinks. I'm *done* with that." But if your friend is struggling with depression, alcoholism, an eating disorder, a big breakup, loss of a loved one, paranoia, OCD, ADD—or any of those other three-letter diseases we've come to know so well—and you bail on her, then it doesn't matter what you tell yourself: You are not a *real* friend.

If a friend were having a heart attack, we wouldn't walk out of the room saying, "Oh my God, I can't believe you're writhing on the floor like a total idiot. This is just not acceptable. You'd better stop that or I'll never speak to you again." But when people are suffering spiritual or emotional illness, we tend to kick them to the curb instead of loving them back to life.

I have two good friends whose twenty-seven-year-old son has been struggling for several years with a heroin addiction. He's been lucky that some of his friends, rather than saying, "It is unacceptable that you came to my house and stole my money," have rallied to his side, checking him into the hospital and doing their best to get him the help he needs. Obviously, these people subscribe to the No Matter What theory of friendship. But I'm sure that 85 percent of his so-called friends don't bother talking to him anymore, because he's a big time-waster.

Well, guess what, everyone we know may at some point end up in the hospital for physical or emotional illness; they'll have heartbreaks and moments of extreme selfishness and even offensiveness. One thing I can promise you is that life will show you its glory, beauty, *and* ugliness—it will raise *all* its heads at some point.

When you think about it, friends who are lost or overextended are really just crying out for help, and they need our friendship and love more than ever. When we see people we know acting in a mean or inappropriate way, we need to move closer to these people. In fact, I believe we should psychically throw them a lifesaver to grab as we pull them back to wellness, family, and heart. We need to treat them as a mother would treat her child.

I don't know about you, but to me it is *such* a relief when I do something completely out of whack and absolutely terrifying and my friend says, "That was completely out of whack and absolutely terrifying, but it's okay. I still love you, and we're going to get through this." In fact, for me this is the feeling of "relief." If you're a conscious human being you're probably already feeling ashamed enough as it is!

I know that over the last year, when I've really been stressed out with work, motherhood, a recession, two TV shows, the death of my father, and promoting a book, I've had some moments of not so nice behavior. A couple of my friends have said, "Are you okay? I am worried about you!" while others have been coy and judgmental, saying things like, "Are you okay? You're acting kind of weird and agitated. That's not cool." To which I want to say, *Duh, of course I'm not okay! I have four jobs! Go fuck yourself, I think I'm handling everything just beautifully!*

One recent evening, I got a text from my friend Jack. Handsome and wealthy, he said he felt unhappy in this world. He's not the type to cry wolf, so without hesitating, I split from a business meeting to run down the street to hug him like a child. He told me that I was the only person in the world he wanted to see in that moment. Four days later, I was hanging at a bar with a friend when he texted me again, asking where I was. When I told him, he showed up with two young girls. This was nothing unusual; being handsome and rich, he's always surrounded by women volunteering to be his wife.

But on this night I was hanging out with a coworker and knew I wasn't in a place to receive these girls. Despite what people may think, at night I really just want to be peaceful, and the last thing I want to talk about is fashion. I'm surrounded for fourteen hours a day by young women, with three phone calls in progress at all times, running from meeting to meeting.

"Do not bring these chicks to our table," I told my friend.

Of course, he ignored me. Soon we were listening to some twenty-two-year-old patter on about how she used to be a model. "Listen," I said. "What kind of model are you?" Let's just say it all went downhill from there. This is why I really recommend you try to stay as conscious as possible—to limit the amount of apology time you have to set aside in your life.

The next day, I called my friend to say I was sorry. I mean, why was I picking on a twenty-two-year-old? It just wasn't nice, and I was not proud of my behavior. Instead of blowing up at me, my friend simply said, "You're so amazing. But the person I called for help last week was *not* the being I was experiencing last night. I just think you're just really overwhelmed, and I'm worried about you."

It's not easy to forgive and move on when you feel hurt or confused by a friend. But offering forgiveness with a heart full of understanding rather than a fist full of resentment is one of the most amazing things you can do for someone—and for yourself.

The meaning of forgiveness has been confused in our culture. It doesn't mean, "I agree with you," or even "I like what you did," or "You didn't hurt me." It means, "I recognize in you the human being in me, and therefore I understand *how* this happened and I'm willing to move forward in my relationship with you. I'd also like to talk about why this happened or is happening, and what I can do to help you." I've had young women in my office who have done something stupid—obviously out of real personal pain—and instead of firing them, I've taken it upon myself to grow closer to them and help them through whatever is holding them back. I'm not saying these people are necessarily in my No Matter What Club. But I do believe we all need help at certain points in our lives, and we appreciate small acts of kindness and understanding.

Once you've made vows of lasting friendship, I hope you'll stand by your friends no matter what they do. Maybe you should even put it in writing, like old-fashioned marriage vows (without the sex):

Do you vow to keep _____ as your friend no matter what, even if she makes a fool of herself in the middle of the night? If you see her escalating, do you promise to go toward her and offer her meditative practices or bring her ice cream? Will you love her when she is not loving you or herself?

If you want your friends to be more forgiving of you, you're going to need to be more forgiving of them, and more helpful. You can also use these opportunities to evolve and grow closer.

I'm not saying we should tolerate unacceptable behavior from everyone or that our No Matter What Club should be a codependent free-for-all bazaar. You have to have boundaries. I don't want anyone to be stuck in a dangerous or violent situation. But we also need to be very careful that we don't use the DSM-V*—a nasty little book that psychologists use to diagnose mental illness (by checking symptoms like "suffers from delusions of grandeur; dry mouth; believes in crop circles"—I mean, this could be any of us on a bad day!)—as a shield to protect us from our own slothlike responses to loved ones in our own community.

---

* Diagnostic and Statistical Manual of Mental Disorders.

If your friend is a drug addict, being abused by her boy-friend, or struggling with an eating disorder, you need to at least sit her down in a quiet and loving manner and say, "I am worried about you. I want to help." If you don't—and you might not want to hear this—I believe you've contributed to her downfall, since it was inconvenient for you and you just couldn't deal. I'm not saying any of us can single-handedly cure anyone of drug addiction or anorexia. But I will tell you one thing:

The truth is one of the most powerful vehicles ever driven by humanity. An arrow shot into a diseased heart can perform a world of wonders.

Even if you need to take your physical distance, I hope you'll stay invested, praying and meditating daily for your loved one—and for everyone else in the world who's suffering while you're at it. In my twenties, when my drug use was spiraling out of control, I coined the phrase, "Duck, here comes my best friend!" (I was on mushrooms and with David Lee Roth at the time. FYI, mushrooms in New York clubs are not a good idea.) You know you're in a bit of trouble when you start avoiding the people who love you most. Years later, after I'd met The Mother and cleaned up, I was thrilled to run into an old friend from those days on the Lower East Side. I hadn't seen him in years, and he probably assumed I was still out of it. I walked right up to him and told him I was fine and that I'd had an amazing spiritual experience that had changed my life. "I prayed for you every day," he said. Hearing this, I felt my heart blow right open, and I knew it was the truth. I also knew his prayers had helped me.

Despite the fact that I know tons of people, my No Matter What Club is actually quite small—as yours probably will be too, when you really start to think about it. Number one is obviously my daughter, Ava. My love for her is unwavering and has the capacity to springboard over the top of any future dysfunction of hers. There's also Ava's nanny, Nana, who has probably done more for me than any other person in my life.

And Ronnie Cutrone, my first husband. Ronnie and I haven't been intimate in decades, but our love has morphed into different forms over the years. Ronnie doesn't have any other family, so I've gone from being his much younger second wife from upstate New York to the executor of his estate and closest of kin. (Years ago, he called me and told me I'd have to share this duty with Tatiana, one of his ex-girlfriends.) I've always known that when Ronnie nears the end, regardless of what's going on in my life, I'll drop everything to be at his side—and that it will ultimately be me who buries him. It doesn't really matter what's happened in the past, because my love for him is bigger than any of our antics.

Then there's my mother, my sister, Allison, and my brother, Lee. Despite the fact that I grew up with all of them, we're completely different. Unlike some families, we don't share political beliefs or any common interests. Take my brother. He's into Nascar; I'm into Margiela. He lives in Virginia; I live in SoHo. Jesus is his God; The Mother is mine. Even though my brother and I don't see eye to eye about things like Michael Moore and politics, I have to tip my hat to him, for he placed me in his No Matter What Club long ago. When we were growing up, it was me who held Lee's hand and told him not to worry at the zoo, that the animals weren't going to bite him. But as we got older, my brother became the leader, and I the loser.

I was just beginning to burn through all my money in L.A., using drugs, and erasing the life I'd built for myself in New York (my first PR business, my friends, my husband), when my brother called to offer his support. He was only nineteen at the time, at the University of Rochester on a hockey scholarship. But he was so obviously distraught over my situation that he burst into tears on the phone and told me he felt I might die. He even offered to cash in his scholarship and come take care of me until I got back on my feet again. I may not have grasped the significance of all this at the time, but if Lee called me in distress today, I would be there as fast as I could. (And yes, Allison, I would do the same for you.)

Unfortunately, not everyone in your No Matter What Club will put you in theirs—in fact, some will probably drop you despite how much you love them. This was the case with a good friend of mine who was a prominent fashion editor in L.A. During our ten-year friendship, we shared each other's horrors and joys, including but not limited to her endometriosis scare, the birth of my daughter, my breakup with my second husband, and her husband's draining her bank account to fund his addictions. I could talk to her about anything. After she got a divorce, she met another guy, a wannabe video director whom only she found really interesting. Our friends all made a point to welcome him into our world, but it soon became clear that this guy was a loser and a user.

Years passed, and we had another mutual friend who discovered while trying to get pregnant that she was riddled with breast cancer. After getting several opinions, it was decided she needed a radical double mastectomy. The night before her surgery, I convened a dinner among friends to toast our friendship and celebrate my friend and her beauty. My fashion editor friend brought along her annoying boyfriend. I was running late to the dinner because I'd been working at a photo shoot all day, and no sooner did I walk in than I heard the clinking of glasses. I assumed it was a toast to my friend who was about to go through one of life's most harrowing experiences.

Instead, the wannabe video director stood up to announce to the table that he and my fashion editor friend had decided to get married. They went on to gush about how they were going to do it barefoot on the beach in Mexico, where an infamous, annoying queen we all knew would officiate at the ceremony. Without really even thinking, I stood up and told my fashion editor friend that I thought this was the most inappropriate thing I'd ever heard. Our friend who was sick looked shocked. (She couldn't defend *herself*, and rightly so!) But by then I'd already established a reputation as a straight talker. I was just being myself, and everybody knew it.

The next day, I called up my friend so we could talk. Obviously, we had extremely different viewpoints on the evening, and some mending was in order on both sides. I didn't really feel I'd overreacted. Hadn't her announcement been *slightly* insensitive?

"*No*," she replied. "It's unforgivable that you said I was selfish for announcing my engagement at the dinner table, and I'm never going to speak to you again."

And she never did. Obviously, she wasn't a believer in No Matter What Clubs, or she would've found a way to process my outspoken moment in the context of our entire friendship and move on. Instead, ten years of triumphs and tumultuousness were flushed down the drain. I'd like to tell you I was hurt—and I *was* slightly shocked—but I understand that people can be close-minded. (Now she's married to that asshole, and I'm so glad I don't have to spend the rest of my life listening to him put every sommelier in L.A. through twenty-five minutes of torture as he pretends he has the money and the know-how to order wine and then watch him disappear when the check comes!)

Often the connection we have with people in our No Matter What Club is forged for reasons we can't explain. Sometimes we feel inexplicably connected to certain people before we even really know them. It's a reflection of where our soul is at and the resonance it has with theirs. Think of your life as a movie. Your soul is going to cast the players it wants to cast, and it won't always tell you why. (It's a lot like a French director, actually!) Sometimes some of the people in your No Matter What Club will turn out to be a real handful. There will certainly be times in your relationships with them when you'll be overwhelmed, afraid, and short on compassion. You don't have to be nice *all* the time. There are some people we love even when all the rules of how to love someone and what's appropriate have been broken.

Take Jimmy, my on-again, off-again boyfriend since 1991. We're both Scorpios, so it would be an understatement to say that we're a tossed salad of oil and vinegar. For two decades, we have loved, fucked, cheated, taught, repeated, hated, embraced, dreamed, daydreamed, swam through Hades, intertwined and flown, and ruthlessly ripped each other apart. If I had a choice in the matter, based on my level of education, my success, and our entire history together, I would *never* love him. It would be that simple. Sometimes I wish I'd never met him and could move forward without any memory of him at all! But despite everything we've done to each other, if he called me tomorrow and said, "I've had a heart attack. I'm at Cedars-Sinai," I'd catch the next flight to L.A. Whether we're lovers, friends, or enemies, Jimmy will always be in my No Matter What Club.

When I met Jimmy in 1991, I was living in a house in L.A. with a couple of notorious power girls at the time, fresh off my divorce from Ronnie. One of my roommates, Alison, was dating Lan from Alice in Chains; another, Marissa, was dating Flea from the Red Hot Chili Peppers. Basically, this house was every girl's dream and every parent's nightmare. Jimmy was a music producer for such bands as the Red Hot Chili Peppers and counted Kurt Cobain as one of his best friends. One night Jimmy showed up at our house with Flea. Jimmy was the quiet guy in the back of the room—the one who attracts girls like a vortex, because they just *know* he can throw down.

(I now interrupt this chapter to bring you my theory on men. The ones who can throw down are like Rottweilers; they don't come running up to you, yapping, and sitting on top of you. Instead, they just stand there and let you feel their presence. The ones who are yapping and talking all the time—well, let's just say they probably have a bigger bark than bite.)

I guess you could say Jimmy and I had an instant connection, but almost every girl has an instant connection with Jimmy. It wasn't long before he became my lover. I joked that I was his three o'clock, between Courtney Love and Juliette Lewis. I usually left his house thinking, *I am never coming back. He does not appreciate me!* Little did I know I'd go on to have this feeling *seven million more times* in the course of our relationship. After I'd met my guru, The Mother, I remember buying a huge smoky quartz crystal and driving over to Jimmy's rock 'n' roll mansion in Hollywood. I'd become convinced that his house was spiritually contaminated, since he abused the feminine there every day. I actually buried the crystal in his front yard as a way to diffuse the negative energies that clearly lived inside. (News flash: Jimmy found the crystal two years ago during a remodel; he couldn't wait to call to tell me.)

In the almost two decades since, Jimmy and I have broken up for years on end. I once even got my nanny to be my partner in a crime against him, ordering her to throw all his stuff into the elevator, so I could chuck it at him while kicking him out of my apartment. (He chose to use this as a yogic experience and sleep outside on Broome Street. He later thanked me for helping him to empathize with the homeless.) When he wasn't infuriating me, he'd have moments of extreme generosity. One time he pulled a $300,000 line of credit out of his house to help grow my business. I cried all the way through the paperwork, because no one had ever done anything like that for me before.

Despite our best efforts, even Jimmy and I—two sweet, but sinister Scorpios—have been unable to destroy this love. For the most part, real love—whether between friends, lovers, family members, or spouses—wants to keep on loving. It can't help itself. Some people describe the Divine as being just that: pure love. My guru, The Mother, once said that when we're in a state of pure love—one that exists on a higher plane than our own petty human emotions—we are in a Divine state. Having a No Matter What Club is really just a way for us to feel what it's like to be Divine, then, to hook up to a force, the Mothership, that none of us could access alone.

In the last fifteen years, there has been so much talk in our culture about what is and is not therapeutically acceptable, and what we do and do *not* have to put up with from other people. Unfortunately, we've left little room for one thing, and that's our human nature. We have so little patience for the things that make us human, and even less understanding of these things. It bothers me that instead of dealing with what's really going on with people or helping them heal, we tend to just recommend they pay someone else to hear about their problems or go on medication. The truth is, most people don't need medication. They need understanding and help.

Take my mom, for example, who was with my father for five decades before his death last year. Growing up, I remember them being deeply into each other—they were partners. When he passed away, my mom was struck down. Her insides were crumbling. Yet when she went to see a doctor, he told her she was depressed and prescribed antidepressants and sleeping pills. When I heard about it, my first thought was, *I'm going to sue this motherfucker!* When the love of your life—the person you've spent forty-two years building your whole world around—is gone, grief is a normal, healthy response! How can anyone want to live in a world where *normal* means crying for a week after your love of half a century dies, but then feeling great because you're on Wellbutrin? This has become normal nowadays. But that's Stephen King's world—that is *not* God's world.

All these medications we're so obsessed with nowadays aren't real solutions; they're just temporary, inadequate aids that separate us from our friends, our personalities, and ultimately our being, constructing a plexiglass shield between our soul and the way we express ourselves. Our soul is put behind a partition, left to mime in vain. Unless you're clinically depressed or bipolar or the kind of person who runs around naked singing "When the Saints Go Marching In" while waving a chain saw, maybe you don't really need to be medicated. Sometimes the easy way out is not the best yogic move. There are plenty of times I too want to medicate myself through my troubles, so I can go through life above the fray, not feeling anything uncomfortable or painful and not offending anyone. There's just one problem: *I'm living!*

At this point in my life, when I call people friends, I pretty much mean that I intend on knowing them for a long time. I may not call them every day, and I may not even see them for a year or two, but I *am* going to be there for them in some capacity if they ever need me. I know that even *I* can't say, "Oh, you have this strange brain disease. I'm going to quit my job and be with you every day," or "You just broke up with your boyfriend? Let me take a week off." We all have to be productive in our jobs and in society. Our lives will always be time-consuming, and there will always be more things that come up with our friends than we can personally handle. But I also believe there is a greater require-ment to true friendship than going to a nightclub a couple times a week trying to score dudes. We need to tend seriously to our friendships on all levels—physical, social, emotional, psychic, *and* spiritual, and in fact if we see a breakdown in any of these elements, we need to step up our game. *Swoosh!*

EIGHT

SEASONS IN THE SUN

I cannot think of death as more
than the going out of one room into another.
—William Blake

Let me tell you something. All the people you love are someday going to die. I've already lost three of the people I've most feared losing: my grandparents and my father (Ava and my mother are the other two; I don't fear my own death anymore). But it was only last year, at my father's deathbed, that I finally *got* it.

Death is like birth, and the soul entering the body and leaving it are equally beautiful and celebratory events, filled with work. When you die, your soul is literally in labor, trying to separate itself from the body and move on to its next phase. (Like giving birth, it can take a while.) Rolling Ava around SoHo in her stroller when she was a baby, I'd often bump into elderly people being pushed in their wheelchairs by caretakers, and it was hard not to notice that the beginning and end of life have a lot in common. We don't have teeth or hair, and we rely on someone else to meet our physical needs.

My question is, why don't we celebrate these life events with equal sincerity? The normal way of celebrating death in our culture is to deny or outright avoid it. It's unfortunate that physical death—the one thing guaranteed us in this world—also happens to be most people's greatest fear. I'm evolved enough to know that my physical body can die at any minute, and that spiritual practice is no guarantee I'll live to be ninety-four. Sometimes the good really do die young, and sometimes evil motherfuckers die old. Most people are afraid of what happens at the end, so they try not to think about it; they don't want to see dying people, and they shield their children from them. They refuse to acknowledge that from the moment we're born, "death is stalking us," as the philosopher Carlos Castaneda wrote.

But if anything, my father's death made me realize that loved ones' deaths should be VIP events! Let's think about this. How many times have you been invited to a great birthday party, a really fun wedding, an engagement party, or a baby shower? Well, when was the last time you received an invite to some-body's *death*? There are so many events in our lives that we're programmed to celebrate, but we've left out one of the most important and certainly the most profound. My loved ones' deaths are some of the most meaningful times I've spent on this planet, certainly more important than breaking the record at Bryant Park for most fashion shows produced in a single day or becoming a bestselling author. It's at my loved one's death-beds that I've experienced the greatest amounts of vulnerability, truth, understanding, forgiveness, empathy, and love; in these moments, I've felt the intimacy we are all starving for as humans. Being present at another person's death isn't anything scary; in fact, it's an honor and a privilege, a sacred and vulnerable experi-ence. It's a rite of passage, and you learn a lot.

I request your presence at my deathbed,
because I love you and honor the time we've shared.
Please join me, won't you, and don't be scared.
Love, Kelly
Date: to be determined. Dress code: black.
Please RSVP to lastdays@peoplesrevolution.com.
This invitation is nontransferable and admits one.

As souls pass into and out of the body, the charms and riddles of the universe are subtly illuminated, and lessons are effortlessly integrated. Just being in the room when loved ones are born or die bestows upon us an understanding of things that words cannot explain—and it's in these inexplicable things that the true and real magic of life lives.

I am suggesting that we treat our death and those of our loved ones the way we'd treat a very special wedding or birthday, i.e., with careful planning and production. By this I don't mean we should plan *how* we'll die—I refuse to attend funerals of suicide victims—but what will happen as we are dying, and *after* we die.

I'm a publicist, so I'll tell you right now what makes for a great event. First, you need a venue. Where will you be? If you're in a hospital, will you be in a private or shared room? What type of music will be played? What kind of drugs will you get? (It's no different than an open bar at your wedding, except this time you won't have to pay the bill!) Perhaps you also want a theme, great lighting, and visuals.

Oh, do you think I'm being morbid? No, I'm being practical. I mean, when you have a baby, there are birthing rooms, classes, soundtracks. Unfortunately, this chapter is probably the closest you'll get to a cool death class, so listen up. I want you to think about this not just for yourself, but also for the ones you love.

A cautionary tale. As my father lay dying last year in Virginia, wheezing in bed and looking like a dead branzino on ice in a fish market, one of his hospice nurses waltzed in and said, in a thick Southern accent, "Lee, you're still here, that must mean Jesus still has work for you to do!"

Hearing this, I dragged her out into the hallway by her arm. "You know what Jesus wants my father to do?" I said. "He wants him to die. *Stop doing this to him.*" I really suggest you get a great door person at your death to avoid this (my father hadn't appointed me, but luckily, I happened to be there to do the honors).

Why leave anything to chance just because you don't yet know the exact date of your last great event? I do want everyone to live a very, very long life. I just think that when the time comes, there should be a clear list of who's allowed to be present and for how long. Who do you want there, and who do you not want there? Who have you told this information to? I get it. I wear all black, I'm forty-five and a Scorpio. But if someone called me to say, "Listen, I don't know where you're going to be in this world when I die, but I want you to know that you're invited to be there"—well, that's one of the sexiest things anyone could ever say to me.

The truth is, I don't think it's ever too early to think about these things, whether you're sixteen, twenty-one, or sixty-one. You may be in perfect health, but do you ride a bike in New York City? Well, what happens if you smash into the cement head-on?

To what lengths do you want doctors to go to keep you alive? And if you don't make it, who will be speaking on your behalf at your funeral, and will you and your God be properly represented? We shouldn't just ask these questions of ourselves, but also of our mothers, sisters, and our tribal elders. We need to organize tribal counsel meetings with our parents, our grandparents and partners.

We live in a time when everyone is silently texting all day, but we're not connecting enough as human beings and having the important conversations. Planning our deaths, like the deaths themselves, is a beautiful opportunity for truth, intimacy, and vulnerability. We all have a bakery number with our name on it, and it's better to acknowledge that now and spend a couple hundred bucks downloading a living will for everyone in the family than to wait until we or one of our parents gets sick.

If you don't have a living will, you are a stupid motherfucker.*

Being in control of our lives until the very end is being responsible and independent, and it is free.

MILLIE, BILLY, AND A MERCEDES HEARSE

> Good-bye, Papa, it's hard to die
> when all the birds are singing in the sky.
> —From "Seasons in the Sun," by Terry Jacks

I used to think death was terrifying too, if I ever thought about it at all, which, growing up, I really didn't. Who *did*? My biggest problems before my grandfather got sick were why my

---

* Visit CaringInfo.org to download one for free for yourself and your family members.

boyfriend wasn't calling me back and how I was going to repay my student loans. These, to me, were life's big issues. But at the age of nineteen, I suddenly and with little warning found myself at my grandfather's deathbed in Syracuse. I was a nursing student at the time, which meant I was often on rotation at the hospital where he was battling throat and lung cancer. No one in my family had ever died before, so watching him deteriorate was scary and confusing, to say the least. As he got sicker and sicker, I realized he was going to be my teacher on the big mystery subject of death. This man, whom I loved more than anyone else in the world, who had always been my biggest fan, would illuminate this secret and veiled world for me. He would show me how to help him die.

After a few days of bedside vigils, his doctors made it clear that my grandfather would be taking the Exit Door. Hearing this, I sat with my grandmother for an hour before calling my parents in Virginia to tell them to come right away. My mother muttered that it was snowing out and this *had better be the real thing*. Once she assured me she was on her way, I decided to go meet my friends at a club to blow off steam, since I'd been sitting at my grandfather's bedside for over thirty-six hours. Though he hadn't spoken or moved in hours, my grandfather suddenly sat straight up in bed like a zombie and said, "Millie, she's got pins in her ass, I tell you! Pins in her ass! She can't sit still even when I'm dying!"

Lesson number one: people who are dying can hear you.

The next morning, I was again at my grandmother's side when my parents arrived from Virginia. And sure enough, as they walked into the room, my grandfather sat straight up in his bed again—after fourteen hours of total silence—and said, "Beverly, Lee, what the hell are you doing here?" Naturally, my mother accused me of being dramatic, since I clearly had nothing better to do than prank them from the hospital, where my grandfather was on his deathbed. *NOT!*

The next afternoon, I walked into my grandfather's room to see that the nurses had left him naked in bed, the sheets pulled back from his body to reveal a skeletal frame with a catheter coming out of his penis. This set me on fire. I didn't really have a lot of life experience at this point, but I did have a sense of dignity and tribal acknowledgment, and I couldn't believe anyone would just leave my greatest tribal elder like that. *My* grandfather, *my* medicine chief, who had from the time of my birth treated me nicer than anyone else in my life has to this day, who had always assured me I was his favorite granddaughter, even in the presence of his other grandchildren, and even proved it by letting me use his credit card to buy clothes. (Not to mention cash. He'd distract my grandmother somehow—"Hey, Millie, can you get me a glass of water?"—and then slip me $100. Between 1977 and 1987, that added up to a lot of money.) This was the man who had essentially given me the ability to love and respect men.

I demanded to see the head nurse and told her that that was *it*. We were taking my grandfather home. She threatened me, telling me I had to sign an AMA document (meaning you are removing the patient from the hospital "Against Medical Advice"), which is what doctors use to protect themselves from lawsuits. I didn't care. Here's another universal truth: Italians prefer to die at home. Boom-basta-*done*.

When we got home to my grandparents' house in Syracuse, I immediately made my grandfather a really cool red terrycloth headband with two leather strips that I iced and tied around his head when he was spiking a temp. With his white hair and flannel pajamas, I told him, he looked like a cross between Willie Nelson and Axl Rose, as styled by Ralph Lauren. He didn't say much—how could he? He had no idea what the fuck I was talking about! But when he did speak, it was usually about the World Wrestling Federation (WWF), which he was really into. "Rowdy Roddy Piper!" he'd chant. He hadn't been home long when Italians started arriving with food, mostly cold cuts and cannolis. That's how you know the end is near—when the cannolis and pepperoni start piling up! It was just two days after his return that my grandfather called my grandmother into his room.

"Hey, Millie," he said.

"Yes, Billy," she replied.

He kissed her, allowed a single tear to fall from his eye, and an hour later he was dead.

Now, I don't mean to sound romantic, but I don't know what else anybody could fucking want in life than to die like *this*. Never mind the clothes in our closets and the cars in our driveway—this, to me, is an example of real abundance, truth, and love.

When the dying become the dead, some cultures really get their groove on. The Balinese, for example, know how to throw a funeral. They build a huge Trojan horse out of wood to hold the body and the soul, and then the men serenade it with musical instruments before spinning it in circles and walking for two or three miles to the next village, where they burn the horse (the spinning is so the soul can't find its way back).

Unfortunately, a Sicilian funeral is sads-ville. In fact, it makes Emily Dickinson and Edgar Allen Poe look positively light-hearted. There are two days of viewing the body, followed by the burial; all these days involve cold cuts, cousins, and resentments that have lasted for decades. Black is the preferred color, and the widow is encouraged to wear it with a veil for a year afterwards. It functions almost like a gang symbol—she is a new member of the Widows' Club! At the burial, a priest reads a bunch of prayers, both for the soul and the living, and everyone cries and tosses a flower—usually a rose—onto the casket. In those days, the males in the family also shoveled dirt on top of the casket before it was swallowed by the earth.

As my grandfather was lowered into the ground, it dawned upon me for the first time that *I* was going to die someday too, and that life is a plank of mortality. As my grandfather headed off of it into the ocean of the unknown, my mother stepped up into position, a soon-to-be grandparent, and I stepped up behind her, a soon-to-be wife and mother. Someday, if I were lucky, I'd be the person at the end of the plank, with all my younger relatives still behind me, including my own child, perhaps by then a mother herself. Watching my grandfather descend into the ground, I literally threw up and passed out. (The great thing about being at an Italian funeral is that when you throw up and pass out, everyone is prepared with smelling salts.)

While my grandfather was dying, his biggest concern was obviously who would take care of his beloved, my grandmother, on a daily basis. In fact, one day he looked me in the eye and said, "Kelly, I need you to promise me you're going to take care of your grandmother." Carmela Barnello Petrocci, whom everyone called Millie, was seventy-two when my grandfather died. They'd been married fifty-four years; she'd never even had sex with anyone else. Of course I agreed.

The morning after we lowered him into the ground, I was a little shocked to find her standing in the kitchen, impeccably dressed from head to toe. It was the day the cannolis and pepperoni finally stopped flowing and the relatives left, and there she was, looking like Jackie Kennedy going to a luncheon.

"What are you doing?" I asked her.

"I'm going to see Billy," she replied.

She hadn't realized that the viewing was over—she thought maybe she could go see him in the casket again. I knew right then that if my grandmother could get up every day for the rest of her life and go visit her dead husband, she would. She was all dressed up like a sixteen-year-old girl waiting for her new boyfriend to take her to the dance.

Even then, I meant what I said, so I showed up for my grandmother. In fact, I moved into the upstairs apartment in her two-family home in Syracuse. When you are in your truth, good things happen to you. So although I was technically looking after my grandmother, the laws of reciprocity were in full effect. I now had cable TV, a chef downstairs, and a human alarm clock who would wake me up for school by simply banging on her ceiling with a broom! On top of that, I had my grandmother's love.

I don't want you to think of my grandmother as a frail, incompetent human being. She was actually very strategic. There were lottery tickets to buy and specials at discount grocery stores to take advantage of. One day when she was attacked by a purse thief while strolling to the bank to deposit her Social Security check, she promptly slugged him with her purse and screamed for help! Luckily, the police apprehended her attacker.

This was a great day for my grandmother, most of whose excitement came from naps, cable TV, and gossip she received while attending her friends' funerals. (At one point she said to me, "It's no fun getting old. The only time you see your friends is at funerals.") She went to court, and when the defense attorney questioned her ability to ID the suspect, she scolded him: "Now you listen to me, young man, when someone tries to steal your bag with your Social Security check in it, you're going to remember his face!" This performance landed her a feature in the *Syracuse Herald-Journal*.

Years later, after I'd moved out of my grandmother's and started my business in New York, there was a period of eighteen hours that no one could reach my grandmother—which, in Italian American life, is a long time to not be in contact with your mother. My mother called my grandmother's friends and ultimately the police, who busted down her mahogany door and found her sleeping in a white nightgown, her arms crossed. At first, they weren't sure she was breathing. Of course, she shot straight up in bed and demanded, "What are you doing in my home?" For months afterward, she made it really clear that you'd better not try to take a nap in the middle of the day in this family, because they'd try to bury you!

There eventually came a time when it was no longer a false alarm, and my grandmother was about to pass. My mother and I decided to meet in Syracuse and be with her as her death coaches— just as I'd later hire a birth coach for the arrival of my daughter. So there we were, three generations of women, the younger two encouraging the oldest to push and move, not to welcome a new soul to the planet, but to see one on to its next phase.

I'd hastily stuffed my rental car with file folders as I left New York, and I proceeded to run People's Revolution North out of my grandmother's over-the-top dining room for three weeks, surrounded by bright turquoise walls, a cream yellow Louis XIV table, and an imposing, crystal-encrusted wall piece that was somewhere between a sconce and a chandelier. In the meantime, more cannolis and cold cuts arrived, and with them, relatives.

For days, I bathed and fed my grandmother, who had since my grandfather's death been living mostly in his bathrobe, which she tied with one of his neckties or a hot pink curtain tassel (it was her version of a smoking jacket). At one point while I was bathing her, I saw that her breasts looked like thin, flattened fruit roll-ups.

"Grandma," I said, "we're going to have to get you a boob job!"

"Honey," she replied, "these boobies fed your mother, and they made beautiful love to your grandfather for fifty-four years. I don't need them anymore."

Forget Keats, forget Emerson; this was one of the most poetic and beautiful things I have ever heard, and from a woman who'd never graduated from high school!

Just so you know, most people choose to die alone. When my grandmother passed, I was sitting in the dining room. My

Uncle John, standing in her doorway, saw her leave her body and came to tell us. My mother recoiled and was adamant that she didn't want to see her mother in that state, and in fact she didn't want to leave the kitchen at all, so I immediately called my mother's cousin Donny, owner of Pirro Brothers Funeral Home, and arranged everything. Sometimes when we're adults, we need to allow our parents the opportunity to be children—we need to become the parent of our parent. Yes, it's moments like these when it's time for you to suck it up and take care of shit.

When the end came for my grandmother, I was a different person than I had been when my grandfather passed away sixteen years earlier. I had significant life experience and, more important, my belief system was in place. I'd lost several friends, had a couple abortions; I'd met The Mother, discovered Eastern meditation, and knew that death was not the end, but merely a snap, blink, and great transition—a leapfrog jump into the known of the unknown, if you know what I mean.

As I watched my cousin Donny's men carry my grandmother out of the house in a splendid purple velvet body bag toward his new Mercedes hearse (being family, we got the VIP funeral treatment), I waved good-bye to her from the same window where she'd stood and waved good-bye to me for thirty years, tearing up each time like she'd never see me again. I remember that moment like it was yesterday.

It's times like these when tribal life and ritual—these concepts that humanity, despite ten thousand years and countless different civilizations, religions, wars, and scientific advances, still holds on to, such as taking care of the dying and discarding our loved ones' bodies—bestow teachings we simply can't explain, not in English or even French or Sanskrit. People can write millions of books analyzing their ideas about life and death, but we can only talk *around* the most profound moments; we cannot speak *of* them. I didn't know at the time that my mother would become a grandmother herself within a year, since I would soon get pregnant with Ava as I weathered my second divorce. But I did know, as my mother did also, that she was now next in line— that we'd all taken one more step down the plank.

I had the foresight to perform one last act of service for my grandmother. I marched over to the funeral home, where I demanded to meet the hair and makeup people and proceeded to terrorize them. "Do you hear me, *no orange blush*!" I insisted. "I do *not* want to see any teased hair!" You have to understand, in upstate New York you have to be very specific about this. I demanded a nice simple chignon. Then I brought fabric swatches to the funeral home to ensure my grandmother's final look matched her coffin lining. At one point my husband, who had come up right after she died, took me aside.

"This is not a *Vogue* shoot," he said.

"Oh, I agree," I said. "This is something far more important. It's my grandmother's last visual moment on this planet, and I want to make sure she goes out looking great."

S.O.U.L.: SPARKS OF UNDERSTANDING AND LOVE

I would like to tell you that my grandmother's death was the last hard-hitting death I experienced, but it wasn't. In 2010, I buried my father. I'd heard mixed reviews on what it was like to lose a parent. In yoga, to not have parents is to be free. But it's still undeniably disconcerting to go back to the house you were raised in as you get older and see your parents with new eyes. When you're young, your parents are everything: your government, your God, your food supply, your bank. Over time, they become actual complex and fallible human beings, which can seem very confusing and very Dada (pardon the pun). It's almost as if the Wizard of Oz becomes the Lion or the Tin Man.

In the last years of his life, my father went from being the omnipotent, all-knowing Leland Level Blanding III, the person who took care of everything, to the person who needed taking care of himself. Instead of calling the shots, he was now *getting* them, from my mother, who did not take her marriage vows lightly. (Another word to the wise: you'd better be really nice to your partner when you're young, because if you're not, your later years will be hell!) But one thing I also realized at my father's death is that people are people. We might call them mother, father, brother, sister, lover, husband, or enemy, but at the end everyone's just a person, a fleeting incarnation of a soul that will someday disappear as suddenly as it arrived. One way to think of a soul is as a Spark of Understanding and Love.

All of us are sparks, and the whole global universe is a fireworks show. How does *your* spark manifest in the world? Is it progressive or effective? And what will it leave on this earth when it has moved on?

It could be a child, a company, a book, a piece of legislation you wrote, some other legacy of your creativity, or maybe just the granddaughter who grows up feeling loved and special because you took the time to call her every day. My father was one of six children. Placed in an orphanage at the age of nine, he was a noncompliant, bad-ass, truth-telling punk (sound familiar?). But he ultimately became a loving husband, and his spark with my mother produced three children. Here was a man who had no reason in the world to hope for a relationship—but my parents always loved each other as much, if not more, than they loved us kids, and they always had a healthy sex life. Ultimately, my dad got a lot right. I realized at his death that if you die in your own, noninstitutional pajamas, whether they're designer silks or Target flannel, in your own bed, whether it's a hospital bed or the most expensive Swedish mattress, and you have at least one person who loves you and is not being paid to be there, then this is a high death. No matter how rich or loved you are, there is probably no better way to go.

For me, the experience of losing my father started when I was invited to speak at the Savannah College of Art and Design, a very prestigious art school in Georgia. As my visit to Georgia drew near and the demands on my time intensified, I considered canceling. Why had I agreed to give two talks in Georgia—one at the Savannah campus, and one at the Atlanta campus—for free?

Not long before I was due to depart, I got a phone call from my mom. My dad, who had been battling emphysema for eight years, had taken a turn for the worse; they weren't sure he'd live through the day. All of a sudden it made sense. I'd psychically agreed to take this terribly inconvenient trip to Georgia, so I'd be a quick one-hour plane flight from Virginia when my father's time came. On the Saturday night before my trip, I called him to tell him I felt like I may not see him again.

"You know what, honey?" he said. "I'm proud of you. Your show is great, your book is great."

He sounded upbeat and lucid. Then seventy-four, he'd been bedridden since Ava's birth in 2002, when he'd made it to New York to meet his newborn granddaughter. Soon after that he'd been given three months to live, and we'd dutifully attended his "last" Christmas for seven years, shipping Ava's presents down to Virginia and then hauling them back up to New York. Through it all, my mother, Beverly, had been his devoted caretaker, even though it basically confined her to the house too. (FYI, you know how they say, "Smoking kills"? Well, they mean it.)

When I left my office to catch my plane, I told my staff, "You watch. I'm going to get to Georgia and my dad's going to die."

The morning of my talk in Savannah, I was told that 475 students were gathered to hear me speak, one of the best turn-outs ever for a speaker. As I sat at a faculty lunch before the talk, my mother called again. *Here we go*, I thought. "Your father isn't doing well," she said. I told her there were nearly 500 kids waiting to hear me speak. "Do what you have to do, and call us afterwards," she said.

I walked onto the stage. I have no memory of what I said. I just remember being conscious that my dreams were attacking me. That's the weird thing about dreams—as soon as you start to manifest them, they turn on you, forcing you to rebuild and fortify your belief systems.* By now I had so many of the things I'd

---

*I used to think my dreams would be a plateau where I'd live. But dreams get the Divine excited, because it knows you'll change yourself to achieve them; and after all, the things we want are usually things we need to become.

always wanted, both professionally and personally. But all these things I teach, about the soul, about the physical body being just a cage, were about to be *really* tested. Did I fucking believe in all of my shteeze?

I finished speaking and called my dad. "You need to go," he said, urging me not to cancel my second talk in Atlanta. "Finish your work. I'll see you soon."

I did as he said and then caught the next flight for Virginia. When I arrived at my parents' condo, I offered to take the night shift. For nine days, I sat up with my father, hoping he would die. I'll be honest. I wanted my father to die when I was sitting with him, since my grandparents hadn't. I even contemplated killing him myself. It would've been *so* easy to step on the oxygen tube that was keeping him alive. When you're dying of emphysema, you can't breathe on your own. And it seemed like the right and loving thing to do. His eyes were silver, he was no longer communicating, and I'm sure that nurses and loved ones do it all the time.

But I stopped myself, because, despite what I could see happening on the outside, I had no idea what was going on in his inner world. I didn't know if he was still processing things or why he was still here. (I could also see myself, on my future talk show, accidentally confessing my crime or, worse yet, having a psychic as a guest. I could even see the headlines: "Talk Show Host Admits Killing Her Father!") Instead, I just sat there and watched and listened as death stalked him and he said funny things like, "Sergeant Blanding. Sergeant Blanding, reporting for duty!" (He'd served in the Korean War.) When I started laughing, he said, "Miss, if you

don't mind me saying so, you have an infectious laugh and won-
derful breasts." I mean, I've always wanted to talk to guys about
my boobs, but my dad has never been one of them.

Here's another thing I learned from my father's death—one
I want you to learn too. You have to be very clear about whether
you want medications at the end and what kind of treatments
you're willing to undergo to keep you (or your loved ones) alive.
My father had a "Do Not Resuscitate," which meant he didn't
want to be resuscitated by machines if his heart stopped beat-
ing. But he was still on oxygen, which was keeping him alive—
artificially! I also noticed his nurses were giving him Haldol, an
antipsychotic medicine most often given to schizophrenics and
patients with Alzheimer's. When I asked why, they said, "He
seems anxious and confused."

"Fuck you," I said. "He's not anxious and confused. He's
dying!"

Ten days after we arrived, my father was no longer speaking
(but he was breathing, compliments of the oxygen). Ava and I
left for New York City. She had to get back to school, and I was
scheduled to fly to L.A. to produce a *Nylon* magazine event—of
all things—with Zac Efron and Vanessa Hudgens.

"Just watch," I said to the kids in my New York office. "*Now*
my father's going to die."

In fact, I was in my closet with my assistant packing my bags
when my sister called, crying. I could feel my assistant looking at
me, thinking, *Oh dear God, please, please tell me that's not your sister.
Don't tell me he's dead. I do not want to be the one in the room with you.
I have done* everything *for you. Don't make me do this. Please do not*

freak out. Please, please, please. He looked like he was bracing to be hit by a tidal wave.

"My father is dead," I told him calmly. "But I am not going to lose my shit. Everything will be all right."

I immediately called my teacher in India for advice. He told me to take the flight to L.A. I got a car to the airport and called my nanny, Nana, to tell her to get Ava out of school and on a plane to L.A. as fast as possible.

When I arrived at the airport, I was informed by the woman at the Delta counter that there was no way I'd make my flight, since I was eight minutes late for check-in. For the first time since my father had taken a turn for the worse, I started crying. I cried and cried, and I was definitely *not* outside. Out of nowhere, two more Delta employees appeared, both very large African American women.

"*Girl,* is that *Kell on Earth*?" one asked. "Didn't she write that book about crying outside, and now she's crying inside!"

They asked me what was wrong, and I explained that my father was dead, but that I was flying across the country in the wrong direction to put on an event with Zac Efron, and now I'd missed my flight check-in by eight minutes.

"Her daddy just died, and you're not letting her on the plane?" exclaimed one of the women accusingly to the ticket agent. "You are *heartless.* She's famous."

Who was I to argue? I put on my black sunglasses, and the two women ushered me through the airport, accompanying me through security to my gate and making sure I had the best seat. Sitting on the plane, relieved and drained, I felt like a layer of my existence had been peeled off. I was about to fly to L.A. and attend a party, while the rest of my tribe was retreating to grieve. Was I really going to work?

But I also knew that, as a yogi, I needed to put my belief systems into action and suck it up. If I really believed the physical body was not the soul, and that my father's soul was levitating with my jet as we lifted above the runway, then why would I allow myself to be paralyzed with grief? Why wouldn't I continue the work that had made my father proud and that was supporting my daughter, his lineage? At the moment of takeoff, I imagined him moving physically and psychically in the same direction as the plane, from the earth to the sky.

My daughter arrived that evening to meet me at the event. The good news was she got to meet Zac Efron. But later in our room I told her that her grandfather, "Da"—who had always called her his "downtown girl" and taken it upon himself to be the premiere loving male figure in her life—was dead. Ava howled like a cross between a baby whale and a wolf.

We flew to Virginia *again* the next day. By now I've seen a lot of people die, and I can tell you that having children or money or fame is no guarantee that anyone will be at your death. At the scene of my father's death, we found my two siblings, their children, and my mother, who had morphed from a conservative 1950s housewife to something else entirely.

"Now let me tell *you* something," she said to us. "My husband is dead, and this is my house, and we are going to do what *I* want."

All of us—my sister, Allison, my brother, Lee, our kids, me—felt our jaws drop.

"We are not going to church," she continued. "We're going to have a celebration of life ceremony. We will put your father's ashes on the table, we'll have Father Jim come to the house, and we'll all stand around talking about what we liked about your father."

The message was clear. Allison, no more hysterics. Lee, no more bullying, and Kelly, no spewing liberal dogma. We would celebrate my father, and the sparks that created all of us and our children too. There we were, all of his sparks, shining to the rhythm of his love, teachings, and memory.

Not long after my grandfather died in 1986, my mom called me to say she was worried we might need to move my grandmother to Virginia to be closer to her. The problem? She wouldn't stop talking to Billy, her dead husband, in the dining room every day. "She thinks he's really there," my mom whispered. I told her I agreed that we should move her, on one condition—that my mother could prove that my grandmother *wasn't* speaking to my grandfather. Well, this story later proved yet another reason we should not point our fingers at our tribal elders.

When my mom walked down the plank of life herself and became a seventy-one-year-old widow, she also missed her lover, and she too started speaking to him every day in their home. In fact, if you ask my mother, he's still living on the second floor. So I'm very aware of the fact that my daughter is watching to know how I behave toward my mother, and I'm encouraging my mother to continue her relationship with my father. To be honest, this is where my yogic training has given me an edge over my siblings—in being able to embrace my mother as a *woman*, and not just as my mother. She's just another beautiful young woman who fell in love with a really great guy who rocked her world, brought out the best and worst in her, and fathered her kids who eventually grew up and left the house, leaving the two of them alone together yet again. At death, we see this kind of panoramic view of life—I saw my mother not just as an old woman, but as a little girl. I saw her as the teenager, as the lover, as the mother, and as the grandmother, all simultaneously, in a gorgeous kaleidoscope view of the feminine. And I knew I was just another kaleidoscope looking at her.

When I was in Ireland recently, I found her a Victorian necklace. She can unscrew its small capsule and fill it with my father's ashes, so she can keep him close to her heart. This way, she and her lover can leave the house together.

The Appointment in Samarra

(as retold by W. Somerset Maugham, 1933)

The speaker is Death.

There was a merchant in Baghdad who sent his servant to market to buy provisions. In a little while the servant came back, white and trembling, and said, Master, just now when I was in the marketplace I was jostled by a woman in the crowd, and when I turned I saw it was Death that jostled me. She looked at me and made a threatening gesture. Now, lend me your horse, and I will ride away from this city and avoid my fate. I will go to Samarra, and there Death will not find me. The merchant lent him his horse, and the servant mounted it; he dug his spurs in its flanks, and as fast as the horse could gallop he went. Then the merchant went down to the marketplace. He saw me standing in the crowd, and he came to me and said, Why did you make a threatening gesture to my servant when you saw him this morning? That was not a threatening gesture, I said, it was only a start of surprise. I was astonished to see him in Baghdad, for I had an appointment with him tonight in Samarra.

EPILOGUE

The truth is, I actually do practice all the things I preach. I really do believe that normal gets you nowhere. After all, from the time I was seventeen my life has been anything *but* normal, from starting a company in my early twenties, to selling everything to become a tarot card reader and living on a yoga mat in Los Angeles, to getting randomly signed to Atlantic Records in my late twenties on a total fluke (despite not being able to read music). Throw in a couple weddings and divorces and ultimately having a child by myself at thirty-five, and, well, *none* of these things is normal.

In fact, it got to the point a few years ago that normalcy started to seem like a really exotic fruit that I really, truly wanted to eat. I had no idea what it would be like to drive my daughter to a ballet lesson or soccer game on a weekday or even to live with the father of my child as a family, to walk down the street hand in hand together. I'd never had the experience of someone coming home at seven and saying, "Hi, honey. Do you want to go out to dinner?" It'd been years since I'd lived with anyone at all! I mean, I think maybe the last movie I saw in an actual theater was the first *Harry Potter,* when I was pregnant and in Montreal on business with Ava's dad. And what can I say, I guess it started to irk me when I'd meet cute, seemingly happy families at my daughter's friends' birthday parties and imagine them wearing matching Snuggies and watching TV on Saturday mornings on the couch. Or when I'd walk by bistros in my neighborhood and see couples having what seemed to be romantic dinners at seven thirty on a weeknight. Let's face it, seven thirty was basically lunchtime for me, and there was nothing romantic about it.

I admit I'd let my schedule get a little out of hand at the time: On a typical day, I'd wake up at seven, meditate, see my daughter off to school by eight fifteen, work, work, work, drink coffee all day, grab a salad at two, work, work, greet Ava when she came home from school, see her at six for her dinner, put her to sleep at nine, get my own dinner at nine fifteen, usually with someone I worked with, and then work until one or two in the morning. I even slept with my BlackBerry under my pillow in case someone called wanting to work in the middle of the night (now, with the recent research on cell phones and cancer, I keep it off but still within reach). I know I've said my work is my yoga, but there was nothing yogic about this schedule. It was more like boot camp for really crazy monks.

And so it was that around age forty even *I* started to envy the so-called normals out there. In fact, I became a little obsessed with normalcy. I wondered what it would be like to fall asleep at night in a home where there was a man to keep me safe. Or to have more time off to walk around the city with Ava or to go for bike rides. I wanted to find out if the relatively easier lives that the people around me seemed to have were as pleasant as they looked. So I started to try to emulate them. I insisted on going out to dinner with nonwork friends. I tried to be open to dating. I went to Home Depot and Michael's craft store. I considered scrapbooking (I eventually decided against it because it seemed like it would take $800 to get my scrapbook going and, frankly, that's a Margiela shirt). Believe it or not, I even strung my whole loft in bright Martha Stewart and Lily Pulitzer tissue paper flowers I put together with Ava; this was the décor for our Easter dinner!

And I didn't stop there. I took a chunk of the money I'd earned on MTV and announced to my employees that we should all start exercising. Then I bought each and every person at People's Revolution a $500 bicycle and christened us the Grand Street Sports Club. We had baskets and bells; we were even featured in the *New York Times* for our riding prowess! I also denounced grocery stores; instead, you could find me throughout the week with the rest of New York City's domestic mavens at the farmer's market, buying good organic produce.

My country house at the time shared a beach on a lake with several other families. I'd always avoided going there during prime sunbathing hours, because I hate group sports. In fact, the words "moms" and "bathing suits" used in the same sentence had always been enough to send me on a rocket to another planet. Instead, I'd go to the lake around eight for an evening sidestroke or early in the morning before anyone else woke up. It had always seemed like my worst nightmare to cart my coolers and beach reads and sunblock down the wooded path at ten on the dot and spend the whole day drinking Sprites and eating cheese balls with everyone else. But in the spirit of normalcy, I even gave *this* a whirl. And you know what? It was painful. I had nothing in common with these people and nothing to discuss with them. I'd never seen *Mad Men* or *The Office;* I'd never been to Atlantis or Cancun. In fact, I felt like I was visiting from another planet.

Although a lot of the other things I tried in the name of normalcy were fun and worthwhile, I ultimately just couldn't get in the groove. This sane and normal life—the same one being lived, give or take a few details, by hundreds of thousands of professional women and mothers in New York—seemed kind of repetitive and animalistic. Get up, exercise, work, eat organic salad greens, drink wine, maybe have sex, go to sleep, and get up and do it all over again. My formerly abnormal life had had its share of repetition too, but at least the grueling work I did was pushing me forward, not keeping me moored in vaguely contented stasis. I couldn't say the same about dodging crazy cab drivers on my morning bicycle ride. Not that there's anything wrong with riding a bike per se or even sunning yourself on the beach—it's just that I was doing these things for everyone else's reasons, not my own. These weren't *my* preferred activities. And they quickly started to seem like a huge waste of time. I didn't feel replenished or exhilarated; I felt exhausted, emotionally and financially. Where was this all *going*?

In hindsight, my awkward quest for normalcy was one of the most humorous explorations I've taken in my life as well as one of the least rewarding. The truth is, not only does normal get you nowhere; normal doesn't do anything for you, or at least it didn't for me. I'd already known the feeling of winning through self-esteem and hard work, and it was much more invigorating than winning the race to conform to everyone else's life plan or the feeling of having held hands, drunk wine, and watched a movie. Don't get me wrong. That kind of thing can be nourishing at certain moments, but it's hard to be effective at changing the world or yourself when you're eating heavy meals at seven thirty every night—I mean, this is probably why France, a magical country, hasn't managed to catapult itself back to being a real world power!

A lot of people say they want to be special, but they don't want to do the work or to occasionally eat crow in order to grow. This was obviously what had set me questing after normalcy in the first place. I hadn't done any drugs or even really drunk in sixteen years; I'd become a champion worker and an accomplished meditator. I was clearly trying my best to go all the way on this karmayogic path I'd chosen. And at times it seemed overrated, or at least like it was making me miss out on things. And it was, The Mother herself warned people off the path of spirituality—she said it was not for the meek. Few people ever manage to commit totally to the Divine, becoming a swami or a prophet, and few commit to darkness either, becoming a Jeffrey Dahmer or a Charles Manson. Most of us dance between the two, with one foot on either side, for our entire lives. These forces are both incredibly powerful and, on the surface, attractive; as one side starts to consume us, we grab the other as a way to balance ourselves. This is what's normal.

Ultimately, I would like "normal" to become equated with "boring." Let's throw "successful" in there too. Instead, let's use words like "conscious," "collaborative," and "creative" (and of course "charming," "charismatic," and "compassionate"). In my early forties, having strived for years to accomplish many of the things I wanted in my life, from creating a business to raising a daughter, I found myself wondering what was left to do, and *be*. The answer, I now know, is to be of service to others. Compassion and true Universal Motherhood start with consciousness—with awakening to what's going on all around us in this world and summoning our courage and creativity to change it.

If normal gets you nowhere, consciousness will get you fucking everywhere, from Bali to Paris to your very own *bloque*. I hope to see you there.

NOTES

1. Mary Ann Glendon, *A World Made New: Eleanor Roosevelt and the Universal Declaration of Human Rights* (New York: Random House, 2001).

2. Glendon, *A World Made New*.

3. Eleanor Roosevelt, *The Autobiography of Eleanor Roosevelt* (New York: Da Capo, 1961).

4. Roosevelt, *Autobiography*.

5. http://www.fordham.edu/halsall/ancient/cicero-friendship.html (retrieved 12/28/10).